ATLAS SHRUGGED

THE NOVEL, THE FILMS, THE PHILOSOPHY

THE ATLAS SOCIETY

ATLAS SHRUGGED

THE NOVEL, THE FILMS, THE PHILOSOPHY

DAVID KELLEY

EDITOR

For more information, visit
www.atlassociety.org

The Atlas Society is a nonprofit organization developing and promoting open Objectivism: Ayn Rand's philosophy of reason, achievement, individualism, and freedom.

The Atlas Society
P.O. Box 7601 #94614
Washington, DC 20044
(202) AYN-RAND
www.atlassociety.org

CONTENTS

THE PHILOSOPHY

PREFACE

A yn Rand's *Atlas Shrugged* is one of the great American novels of the twentieth century. Published in 1957, it continues to sell hundreds of thousands of copies per year. It has inspired millions of readers with its themes of independence and achievement. Its call for freedom has helped create a vibrant movement to promote economic and personal liberty. And it has finally been adapted as a film trilogy.

Atlas Shrugged is a novel of enormous complexity and depth. For one thing, it crosses genres. In literary form it is an epic, a story about the decline of a society and the heroes who set out to rescue it. But it is also a mystery, a love story, a political dystopia, and a novel of ideas; it even has elements of science fiction. The plot, moreover, is a tightly integrated progression of events. The many subplots, parallels, and repetitions at all levels give the novel a highly complex structure. And as a novel of ideas it presents a challenging new philosophy, conveyed through the events and characters but also articulated in epic speeches.

On first reading, one is easily swept up in the story. First-time readers today are also stunned by the eerie similarities with events in the real society around us. But one reading cannot reveal all the riches on offer in *Atlas Shrugged*. Many people go back to reread: to reenter the world Rand created, to appreciate her literary craft, to relive the drama, to enjoy once again the company of the characters, or to study the ideas.

If you are one of them, this guide is for you. The first section is about the novel. Robert Bidinotto, who has written extensively about *Atlas Shrugged* and is himself a novelist, provides an elegant plot synopsis and an analysis of Rand's literary style. To help you navigate, I have also provided a timeline of the events, chapter by chapter, and a list of (I think!) all the characters.

The second section covers the film adaptation: *Part I: Atlas Shrugged* (2010), *Part II: The Strike* (2012), and *Part III: Who is John Galt?* (2014). Joan Carter, associate producer and the wife of John Aglialoro, the man who made it happen, tells the amazing inside story of his twenty-year effort to produce these films. Next there is a list of the principal and secondary casts, and drawing on my experience as a consultant on the project, I address the question of why the trilogy did not have the same cast for all three films. I also share my observations and insights about how the philosophical speeches were adapted for the screen.

In the final section, this book provides an overview of the philosophical ideas. Bidinotto outlines some core tenets of Rand's philosophy ("The Revolutionary Philosophy . . ."), while I elaborate on the moral and political premises in her defense of capitalism ("The Capitalist Ideal"). Galt's speech in part 3, chapter 7 of the novel is Rand's first full statement of her mature philosophical system; I offer a conceptual outline of the 60-page speech. Finally, there is Edward Hudgins's discussion of the parallels between the novel and events in our world.

For me, reading *Atlas Shrugged* was an early step in an intellectual adventure that continues to this day. I hope you'll join me on that adventure. If you find the ideas in the novel and this companion volume intriguing, I invite you to explore them with me. I've included some recommendations of readings and videos at the back of this book. And I encourage you to visit The Atlas Society's website, http://www.atlassociety.org, and join me in person at the Atlas Summit.

DAVID KELLEY

ACKNOWLEDGMENTS

The editor is grateful to the authors who contributed to this book. I wish to acknowledge Walter Peter Brennen for permission to use his sculpture *Atlas Libertas* for the cover; Matt Holdridge for his cover design; the Atlas Distribution Company for permission to publish "The History of the *Atlas Shrugged* Movie Trilogy"; Atlas Productions LLC for permission to use script material and photographs from the films; and Laurie Rice, writer and research assistant at The Atlas Society, for editorial and film-related work on the book. And I thank all the photographers, professional and otherwise, whose work is included, especially professional photographers Juan Carlos Menéndez, who took the pictures of *Atlas Libertas*, and Judd Weiss, for his photos from the set.

DAVID KELLEY

THE NOVEL

ABOUT AYN RAND

ROBERT BIDINOTTO

Novelist and philosopher Ayn Rand was born Alisa Rosenbaum on February 2, 1905, in Saint Petersburg, Russia. Her family lived in a large, comfortable apartment above the drug store her father owned.

From her earliest years, the girl felt alienated from the dark, brooding atmosphere of Russia, but loved the bright world projected in stories appearing in foreign magazines. At age nine she made the conscious decision to become a writer.

In her teens, she discovered the works of great romantic writers such as Victor Hugo and Edmond Rostand. But as her private vision of human potential expanded, the social horizons of human possibility were shrinking around her. In February 1917 she witnessed the first shots of the Russian Revolution from her balcony. Soon, communists seized her father's shop. Almost overnight, her family was reduced to crushing poverty.

Against the growing squalor of Soviet life, the young woman nurtured a burning desire to abandon Russia for the West. She obtained a passport to visit relatives in Chicago and left Russia and her family in January 1926, never to return. She arrived in New York City weeks later, with only $50 in her purse.

After a brief stay with her Chicago relatives—where she selected the pen name of Ayn Rand—she moved to Hollywood. The day after she arrived, she was given a car ride—and a job as a movie extra—by film director Cecil B. DeMille. Soon after, on the set of DeMille's film *King of Kings*, she literally stumbled into the actor who would eventually become her husband, Frank O'Connor.

Over the next decade, Rand worked at odd jobs. In her spare time she mastered English and churned out screenplays, short stories, and a novel. Her extraordinary perseverance and talent eventually paid off with two Broadway plays and the publication of her first novel, *We the Living*.

But the book that made her famous was *The Fountainhead*. Published in 1943, this great novel of American individualism presented Rand's mature portrait of "Man as hero" in the character of architect Howard Roark. Roark demands the right to design and build loyal only to his own ideals and principles. In his long struggle to succeed—a struggle not unlike Rand's own—he eventually triumphs over every form of spiritual collectivism. This novel first presented Rand's provocative morality of rational egoism. It has remained a bestseller for over half a century, selling millions of copies, and it was made into a film starring Gary Cooper and Patricia Neal.

If *The Fountainhead* created controversy, *Atlas Shrugged* fomented a furor. In this gigantic Romantic epic, Rand dramatized the major elements of her challenging new philosophy of "reason, individualism, and capitalism," which she called "Objectivism." This novel was to be the masterpiece of her literary and philosophic career.

After the publication of *Atlas Shrugged* in 1957, Rand turned to nonfiction, elaborating her philosophy in many essays, columns, and public appearances. Her colorful and tumultuous life ended on March 6, 1982, in her New York apartment.

But in the years since her death, interest in her ideas has only increased. Today, she and her philosophy are the focus of books, film documentaries, magazine and newspaper articles, and a growing intellectual movement of scholars, organizations, and publications.

Plot Synopsis
of *Atlas Shrugged*

Robert Bidinotto

Atlas Shrugged is structured in three major parts, each of which consists of ten chapters. The parts and chapters are named, and the titles typically suggest multiple layers of meaning and implication.

The three parts of the book are each named in tribute to Aristotle's laws of logic.

Part One is titled "Non-Contradiction," and appropriately, the first third of the book confronts two prominent business executives, Dagny Taggart and Hank Rearden—and the reader—with a host of seeming contradictions and paradoxes with no apparent logical solutions.

Part Two, titled "Either-Or," focuses on Dagny Taggart's struggle to resolve a dilemma: either to continue her battle to save her business—or to give it up.

Part Three is titled "A Is A," symbolizing what Rand referred to as "the law of identity"—and here, the answers to all the apparent contradictions finally are identified and resolved by Dagny and Rearden, and also for the reader.

The tale is told largely from the point of view of Dagny, the beautiful, superlatively competent chief of operations for the nation's largest railroad, Taggart Transcontinental. The main story line is Dagny's quest to understand the cause underlying the seemingly inexplicable collapse of her railroad and of industrial civilization—and simultaneously, her tenacious, desperate search for two unknown men: one, the inventor of an abandoned motor so revolutionary that it could have changed the world; the other, a mysterious figure who, like some perverse Pied Piper, seems purposefully bent on luring away from society its most able and talented people—an unseen destroyer.

A major subplot follows steel titan Hank Rearden in his spiritual quest to understand the unknown forces that are undermining his career and happiness and turning his talents and energies toward his own destruction.

In the shoes of Dagny and Rearden, we gradually learn the full explanation behind the startling events wreaking havoc in their world. With them, we come to discover that all the mysteries and strange events of the story proceed from a single philosophical cause —and that Ayn Rand poses a provocative philosophical remedy for many of the moral and cultural crises of our own world.

PART ONE: NON-CONTRADICTION

The time is the late afternoon of September 2. The place: New York City. But it's not quite New York City as we know it.

It's a city in the final stages of decay. The walls of skyscrapers, which once towered sharp-edged and clean into space, are cracked, soot-streaked, and crumbling. Hundreds of storefronts, even on once-prosperous Fifth Avenue, are boarded up and empty. Along the littered sidewalks, streetlights are out, windows are broken, and beggars haunt the shadows.

Eddie Willers walks these desolate streets, feeling a sense of dread he can't explain. Perhaps it's the newspapers, which are filled with ominous stories. Factories are closing, and the nation's industrial infrastructure is falling apart. The federal government is assuming dictatorial emergency powers. Meanwhile, rumors circulate about a mysterious modern pirate ship on the high seas, which sinks government relief vessels. . . .

As Eddie approaches the Taggart Transcontinental Building —headquarters of the great railway system where he works as Dagny Taggart's assistant—he ponders the system's latest train wreck . . . the steady decline of its shipping business . . . and the puzzling loss of its last workers of competence and ability. In fact, these days it seems that everywhere, the great scientists, engineers, and businessmen are either retiring or simply vanishing. . . .

Abruptly, a beggar steps from a darkened doorway and asks for spare change. As Eddie digs through his pockets, the beggar shrugs in resignation and mutters a popular slang expression. It's a phrase whose origins no one knows, but which somehow seems to summarize all the feelings of pain, fear, and guilt now gripping the world. The beggar's words give voice to Eddie's own mood of dread and despair:

"Who is John Galt?"

These words open the first chapter and close it, hinting at the basic mystery of the plot. Only at the end of the novel do we realize that the reasons for the disintegrating world, for the disappearing men of ability, and for the motives of men such as the story's villains, all lie in the answer to that single question: "Who is John Galt?"

We meet Dagny Taggart en route to New York by train. She is roused from sleep by the sound of a young brakeman whistling a compelling tune. When she asks about it, he replies casually that it's Richard Halley's Fifth Concerto. She is startled: she knows that Halley had quit composing and mysteriously dropped out of sight after writing only four concertos. She confronts the brakeman on this, and he abruptly reverses himself, saying he misspoke; but Dagny senses that he's trying to hide something.

She returns to her office, the battleground where she is fighting to save the family business that her brother, system president James Taggart, seems hell-bent on destroying. Like the rest of industrial society, her railroad is falling apart as its most talented and able men inexplicably quit and disappear. But while Dagny struggles to salvage dying branches of the crumbling system, from Jim she gets only a bewildering evasiveness, a whining resentment of decision-making responsibility, and furtive hostility toward men of achievement. Over Jim's heated objections, Dagny decides to replace the crumbling Colorado track with new rail made from Rearden Metal, Hank Rearden's untested but revolutionary new alloy. At day's end, she receives an appointment from one of the system's most promising young men, Owen Kellogg. He surprises her by quitting, without explanation, despite her offer to promote him to head the Ohio division. Asked why, he answers only, "Who is John Galt?"

On a deserted road, Hank Rearden walks home from work on the day he has just poured the first heat of Rearden Metal. In his pocket is a chain bracelet—the first thing ever made from the metal: a gift for his wife, Lillian.

Rearden is serenely confident in his work but bewildered by the irrationality of people around him. When he gives Lillian his gift, she and his family mock it as an act of selfishness. This response is nothing new: though dependent on him economically, his family constantly belittle his achievements and values. Yet Rearden silently tolerates their hostility. We are left wondering exactly who is chained to whom, and why.

As he ponders the mystery of his family, family friend Paul Larkin warns him vaguely, almost apologetically, about the loyalty of his Washington lobbyist, Wesley Mouch. Rearden wonders what Larkin is driving at. Unknown to Dagny and Rearden, James Taggart has been conspiring with Mouch, Larkin, and rival steel company president Orren Boyle to use their political pull to pass laws that will crush a competing regional railroad in Colorado and eventually cripple Rearden's steel operations as well.

The destruction of the regional railroad forces Colorado oilman Ellis Wyatt, whose oil fields fuel the nation, to ship with Taggart Transcontinental instead. But the Colorado line of the Taggart system is in total disrepair. Wyatt issues Dagny an angry ultimatum: Either be ready to handle all his freight within nine months, or face economic ruin. "If I go," he vows, "I'll make sure that I take all the rest of you along with me."

Enter Francisco d'Anconia, the brilliant, spectacularly successful owner of the d'Anconia Copper company, and Dagny's former lover. Years before, he had abruptly ended their relationship without explanation. Then newspapers began to report that the incomparable creative genius that she'd once loved had become an irresponsible international playboy.

When Mexico suddenly nationalizes Francisco's San Sebastián copper mines, everyone is stunned to learn that they were empty of copper and utterly worthless. Knowing that Francisco would never make a poor investment, Dagny suspects that he had concocted the whole debacle. When she challenges him about it, Francisco gaily confirms that he had expected the nationalization—and had consciously let himself lose millions, simply in order to ruin his major investors, including Jim Taggart and Orren Boyle. He adds, without elaboration, that his ultimate target for ruin is Dagny herself.

At a wedding anniversary party for Rearden and his wife, Lillian, a pack of prominent intellectuals invited by Lillian loudly damns all the values and virtues that Hank Rearden embodies: reason, independence, self-interest, and pride in productive achievement. Only Francisco d'Anconia, the contemptible playboy, dares to approach Rearden respectfully and thank him for those virtues. Rearden is mystified—yet privately grateful.

When Rearden refuses to sell all rights to Rearden Metal to the State Science Institute, the Institute retaliates with a public statement questioning the safety of the metal. This causes work on the Colorado rail line to grind to a halt. Dagny implores renowned physicist Dr. Robert Stadler, who heads the Institute, to retract the indefensible statement. But Stadler refuses, fearing that a public reversal would put his Institute in a bad light. "What can you do when you have to deal with people?" he says.

To justify his cynicism, he tells her about his three most promising students years ago, when he taught physics at Patrick Henry University. One, Ragnar Danneskjöld, became a pirate who robs government relief ships. A second, Francisco d'Anconia, became a worthless playboy. And the third dropped out of sight, not even making a name for himself, but before leaving, damned Stadler for launching the State Science Institute.

To continue work, Dagny forces Jim to temporarily "sell" her their Colorado branch line as a separate company. She names it "the John Galt Line," in defiance against the widespread despair that the popular catch phrase symbolizes. However, without warning, the conspirators' secret machinations result in a new antitrust law that forces Rearden to surrender ownership of many of his subsidiaries, including his ore mines.

Still, despite enormous opposition and obstacles, Dagny and Rearden complete the John Galt Line before the deadline Ellis Wyatt had given them. To prove the safety of Rearden Metal, they ride in the locomotive on the first run to Colorado. As the train speeds triumphantly across America, the two silently share their victory over years of adversity and irrationality. And with each passing mile, the undercurrent of sexual tension grows between them.

That night, at Ellis Wyatt's home, Rearden's wall of reserve finally cracks, and the two begin a secret, passionate affair. But Dagny is disturbed by Rearden's derisive comments about their immorality. His words suggest an inner conflict yet to be resolved.

They decide to take a vacation together. Driving through Wisconsin towns that have reverted to pre-industrial primitiveness, they visit the empty ruins of the Twentieth Century Motor Company—a once successful factory that had been destroyed by worthless heirs. There Dagny makes a startling discovery: a few remnants of a revolutionary motor that had once converted static atmospheric electricity for human use. But there's no clue as to its inventor, how his machine worked—or why he would have abandoned so monumental an invention.

Upon their return to New York, they find that political pressure groups are clamoring for even more laws to punish success and productivity. While Rearden works feverishly to get the ore he needs, Dagny begins a private search around the country for the inventor of the motor. The trail from the Twentieth Century Motor Company leads her from one parasite to another, until she learns that the inventor had been the brilliant young assistant of the factory's chief engineer. But she can't learn his name.

She goes to a diner where she's been told a friend of the young engineer's works as cook. There, she eats the best hamburger she's ever had—and is amazed to find the man who made it is Dr. Hugh Akston, formerly a great philosopher at Patrick Henry University. He refuses to explain why he left his profession, or his current presence in so lowly a job. He also admits that he knows who invented the motor but refuses to reveal his name. Instead, he tells Dagny that while she won't find him, someday he will find her.

Akston—who, like Stadler, had taught Francisco and Ragnar Danneskjöld at Patrick Henry University—concludes by giving her much the same advice that Francisco once had: If she finds it inconceivable that such a motor would be abandoned, or that a great philosopher would work in a diner, she should remember that contradictions can't exist in nature—and that she should therefore check her premises, because one of them must be wrong.

Returning to New York, Dagny learns of a new series of dictatorial directives. These limit railroad speeds and train lengths, eliminating the advantage of the high-speed Galt Line; limit the production of companies' metal alloys to the average of their competitors' and order them to provide all customers "a fair share" of their

products on demand; and forbid manufacturers from relocating without government permission. A heavy new tax is placed on Colorado industries in order to help needier states. These directives will cripple
Taggart Transcontinental and rob Hank Rearden and the bondholders of the John Galt Line, but—she realizes with horror—destroy Ellis Wyatt.

Dagny remembers Wyatt's grim ultimatum and races by train to try to reach him. But she arrives to find the fields of Wyatt Oil ablaze—and Wyatt's handwritten message:

"I am leaving it as I found it. Take over. It's yours."

PART TWO: EITHER-OR

In the wake of the new directives, the nation's oil industry has collapsed, and like Wyatt, many other Colorado industrialists vanish.

Dagny meets again with Stadler, asking him to read the fragmentary notes left behind by the inventor of the motor in order to try to learn his identity. Stadler is amazed—but angry because the unknown genius had decided to work for industrial applications rather than pure theory, and piqued because the man had never approached Stadler personally to share his path-breaking theories. Stadler mockingly expresses his resentment of practical achievements.

A man nearby mutters, "Who is John Galt?"—and Stadler remarks that he knew a John Galt once: a mind of such brilliance that, had he lived, the whole world would be talking about him.

"But the whole world is talking of him," Dagny points out.

Disturbed, Stadler dismisses it all as a meaningless coincidence. "He has to be dead," he says with a curious emphasis.

The government saddles Rearden Steel with a young spy named Tony, whose job is to watch Rearden for compliance with government regulations. Rearden nicknames the boy his "Wet Nurse." Shortly after Tony warns him about his uncooperative attitude, Rearden is approached again by the State Science Institute—this time with orders to supply Rearden Metal for a mysterious "Project X." He refuses, inviting the Institute to take the metal by force, if they wish. The Institute messenger reacts to this prospect with undisguised horror.

Rearden realizes that somehow, to succeed in their schemes against him, his enemies need his own voluntary cooperation. At the same time, he begins to sense that what he feels for Dagny reflects not the worst within him, but the best.

By now, Dagny has concluded there is a "destroyer" deliberately removing achievers from the world for some inconceivable reason. As for the motor, she hires a brilliant young scientist in Utah, Quentin Daniels, to rebuild it if he can.

Rearden secretly sells Rearden Metal to coal magnate Ken Danagger—a transaction made illegal by the directives. The disturbing thought occurs to him that his only pleasures, at work and in his romantic life, must be kept hidden, like guilty secrets. He wonders why. Meanwhile, Lillian, whom he has ignored for months, begins to suspect that he is having an affair. She demands that he accompany her to Jim Taggart's wedding, and out of a dead sense of marital obligation, Rearden agrees.

Jim has been engaged to a naïve young clerk named Cherryl, who admires him for what she believes is his genius in running the railroad. Jim basks in her blind adulation and maliciously enjoys the awkwardness of her attempts to become socially poised.

Their wedding is attended by a corrupt cross-section of the culturally prominent and politically connected. Mistakenly thinking she is defending a heroic husband against an enemy, Cherryl confronts and insults Dagny. Across the room, Lillian approaches Jim, hinting that her control over her husband is available for trade. Then Francisco enters, crashing the party. After embarrassing Jim, he approaches Dagny, telling her it appears that John Galt has come to claim the railroad line she named for him. Hearing a dowager's remark that "money is the root of all evil," he gives an impromptu speech defending money-making on moral grounds, as a symbol of achievement, free trade, and justice.

Francisco approaches Rearden and admits that his words were intended for him, to arm him morally for self-defense. Rearden is grateful—until Francisco reveals that he's deliberately destroying d'Anconia Copper, precisely to harm the looters who are profiteering on his abilities. Rearden recoils in horror. Then Francisco lets it be known, loudly, that his company is in trouble. As the news sweeps the crowd, many of whom are d'Anconia investors, the wedding party breaks up in panic.

After the party, Lillian confronts Rearden with her suspicion that he's having an affair, presumably with some tramp. Rearden admits to an affair, but refuses to identify his mistress or to stop seeing her. For reasons he can't fathom, though, Lillian refuses to divorce him.

Soon afterwards, Rearden is visited by Dr. Floyd Ferris of the State Science Institute. Ferris threatens him with jail for selling Rearden Metal to Ken Danagger—unless he agrees to sell it to the State Science Institute as well. Glimpsing a flaw in this blackmail scheme, Rearden once again refuses.

In the Taggart cafeteria, Eddie opens his heart to a long-time confidant, a worker of his acquaintance whose name he has long forgotten. He reveals Dagny's suspicions about the "destroyer," her fear that Ken Danagger will be the next to go, and her intention to visit him at once to prevent that from happening.

When Dagny arrives at Danagger's office, he is in a meeting with someone else. After a long delay, the other man leaves, unseen, by the rear entrance—and Dagny enters to find she's too late. Danagger informs her that he's quitting. Like Kellogg and Akston, he won't explain why. She realizes that she's just missed "the destroyer," but Danagger reassures her that nothing she can say would have mattered anyway. Then Dagny spots a cigarette butt in his ashtray: it bears the imprint of the gold dollar sign.

The day after Danagger's disappearance, Francisco visits Rearden at his mills. He begins to explain to him that by continuing to work under these dictatorial circumstances, Rearden is granting a moral sanction to the looters, a sanction they need from him in order to destroy him. In the exchange that gave the novel its title, Francisco asks Rearden what he would tell the Titan Atlas of Greek mythology, crushed by the weight of the world that he bears on his shoulders.

Rearden has no answer. Francisco says he'd tell Atlas to shrug.

Rearden begins to understand—when they are interrupted by a furnace emergency in the mills. They work side by side to resolve the crisis, but the moment is lost; Francisco decides it's not yet time to discuss things further.

At their Thanksgiving dinner, Lillian tries to dissuade her husband from taking the witness stand at his trial the following day, informing him that he has no moral right to protest. But Rearden startles them all by rebuking his brother for insulting him. They notice that he seems to have a new confidence—and he notices that this seems to disturb them. Meeting later with Dagny, he informs her that she'll have all the Rearden Metal she needs, laws be damned.

At his trial, Rearden acknowledges his actions with Danagger —but refuses to accept that they were in any way immoral. Instead, borrowing from Francisco's words, he gives a rousing moral defense of his right to produce for his own sake, bringing the audience to cheers and leaving the judges speechless. Instead of jailing him, they seem panicked—and give him a suspended sentence. Rearden smiles, beginning to grasp the concept of "the sanction of the victim."

Drawn by curiosity about Francisco's incongruous reputation as a playboy, Rearden visits him, finding him working on blueprints. Francisco admits that his reputation has been mere camouflage for a secret purpose of his own. Denying that he has been promiscuous, he explains the moral meaning of sex. But unknow-ingly, he is also addressing Rearden's own private sexual conflicts. Feeling a growing comradeship, Rearden reveals he's just placed a huge, urgently needed order with d'Anconia Copper.

Horrified, Francisco leaps to the phone—then stops. In obvi-ous anguish, he solemnly swears to Rearden "by the woman I love" that, despite what is about to happen, he remains Rearden's true friend.

Soon after, the d'Anconia ships carrying copper to Rearden are sunk by Ragnar Danneskjöld. Rearden is overwhelmed by a sense of personal betrayal. He realizes that Francisco somehow knew of the sinking in advance and could have stopped it—but didn't.

It is Rearden Steel's first failure to deliver an order on time. The delay in the Rearden Metal shipment to Taggart Transcontin-ental starts a devastating economic chain reaction, holding up trains, spoiling shipments of food, forcing farmers to go bankrupt and factories to shut down, causing deteriorating bridges across the Mississippi to close—and leaving the famous Taggart Bridge as the river's last crossing point.

Meanwhile, coal that Taggart Transcontinental desperately needs is diverted to foreign aid, the government censors newspaper stories of the disasters and their causes, and the top floors of build-ings are shut down to conserve fuel. Rearden is forced to make deals with hired gangs to mine coal at night in abandoned mines.

With Colorado industry now in shambles, the Taggart Transcontinental board of directors meets to formally close the John Galt Line. In exchange for permission to shut down the line, a gov-ernment bureaucrat prods them to raise all Taggart worker wages. They try to nudge Dagny into stating openly the final decision to close the line; but—following Rearden's example from the trial—she refuses to help them and grant a moral sanction for their actions by taking the responsibility to venture an opinion. They finally put the matter to the inevitable vote.

Francisco is waiting for her afterwards. "Have they finally murdered John Galt?" he asks softly. He comforts her at a nearby café. Then he asks her why it is that heroic builders, like the railroad's founder, Nat Taggart, have always lost battles with pale cowards such as those on Taggart's board. As she ponders this, he reflects aloud, almost abstractly, about how his ancestor, Sebastián d'Anconia, had to wait fifteen years for the woman he loved. Dagny is astonished at this tacit confession but replies coldly by asking him why he has hurt Hank Rearden. Francisco answers solemnly that he'd have given his life to Rearden—except for the man to whom he had given it.

Later, noticing the familiar question carved in the tabletop, he offers his answer: "John Galt is Prometheus who changed his mind." After being torn by vultures for bringing men fire, Francisco says, Galt "withdrew his fire—until the day when men withdraw their vultures."

In Colorado with Rearden, Dagny supervises the aftermath of the Line's closure: scavenging machines from closed factories, watching towns emptying, seeing refugees crowd the last departing trains.

Meanwhile, eager for more Washington influence, Jim conspires with Lillian to deliver Rearden to the bureaucrats. Lillian finds that her husband is traveling home by train under a phony name, presumably with his mistress. When she meets the train to confront them, she sees him not with some cheap slut, but with Dagny Taggart.

Lillian is devastated—and terrified. She grasps now why her grip on her husband is failing, and simultaneously, his unapologetic demeanor at his trial: Dagny has empowered her husband to reject guilt.

"Anybody but her!" she cries to him in terror. But Rearden is indifferent to her efforts to make him feel guilty or give up Dagny. In Lillian's vile insults against Dagny, Rearden realizes that hers had been his own view of sex. Though Lillian tells him she won't divorce him, he feels at last liberated and guiltless. Still, Lillian senses that he wants the affair to be kept secret—and that, she realizes, may be used as a weapon.

Without warning, the government issues Directive 10-289, a regulatory measure that seizes total control of the entire economy and orders all existing economic arrangements to be frozen in place. All patents on inventions are to be turned over to the government in the form of Gift Certificates. In addition, to stop people of talent from disappearing, the law forbids anyone from quitting his job.

It's the last straw for Dagny, who throws the newspaper into James Taggart's face and resigns. She leaves for the Taggart lodge in the country, letting only Eddie know her whereabouts. But Rearden stays behind, confident that he can dynamite the new directive simply by refusing to comply with the order to surrender his patents to Rearden Metal.

In response to the directive, a mood of quiet rebellion sweeps the nation. Each day, more people fail to show up for work. Even Rearden's "Wet Nurse" is indignant, and vows to look the other way if Rearden chooses to break laws. Meanwhile Lillian mysteriously disappears on a vacation trip.

On a spring morning, Dr. Floyd Ferris arrives at Rearden's mills. He reveals that the government has been tipped off by Lillian to Rearden's affair with Dagny. If Rearden won't sign the Gift Certificate transferring Rearden Metal to the government, Ferris will expose the affair in the media, sullying Dagny's reputation in scandal. Rearden suddenly realizes much more about the motives of his enemies—and about the moral premises that have caused such conflict in his life. But refusing to let Dagny bear the consequences of his own mistakes, he signs the Gift Certificate.

In the wake of these events, Eddie Willers bares his soul to his friend in the cafeteria. He also lets slip that Dagny has gone off to stay at the Taggart lodge.

Furious at Lillian's betrayal, Rearden orders his attorney to get him a divorce and to leave her with no alimony or property. He moves to an apartment in Philadelphia. Walking home from his mills one evening, he is confronted by a man who presents him with a bar of gold. The man reveals that he's Ragnar Danneskjöld. He says the gold represents wealth looted from Rearden and forcibly reclaimed by Ragnar from the looters. Rearden finds that he can't condemn Ragnar for his actions, and he even helps the outlaw elude pursuing police.

At the Taggart railroad tunnel through the Rockies, a waiting diesel engine is commandeered by the government to allow a bureaucrat to tour the country. This leaves only coal-burning engines on the track. Despite a strict system rule against entering the tunnel with a smoky coal-burner, plus the fact that the tunnel's signal and ventilation systems are malfunctioning, a politician demands that his own train be allowed to proceed through. All the responsible supervisors have quit the Colorado division, leaving decision-making authority to incompetents. Bullied by the politician, each in turn—from James Taggart on down—passes the buck, leaving the final decision to proceed to a green young dispatcher. Abandoned by his superiors, the boy signs the order for the train to enter the tunnel. Miles inside, the crew and passengers are overcome by fumes—and a military train loaded with explosives rushes into the tunnel from the other end. They collide in a cataclysmic explosion that destroys the tunnel.

At the Taggart lodge, Dagny receives a surprise visit from Francisco. He tells her why she was right to quit—and reveals that, for the same reason, he has deliberately been destroying d'Anconia Copper since the night he left her, twelve years before. Dagny begins to see Francisco in a new light—when the radio abruptly brings news of the tunnel explosion. Horrified, she abandons Francisco and rushes back to New York.

After a grueling day dealing with the emergency, Dagny returns to her apartment, where she is visited once again by Francisco. By now she is immune to his arguments but aware that he's part of the "destroyer's" conspiracy. Suddenly the door opens—and

Hank Rearden is standing there, the key to Dagny's apartment in his hand.

Rearden demands to know why Francisco is present. Francisco realizes—and accepts—that Rearden is Dagny's lover. Enraged by what he believes has been Francisco's betrayal of their friendship, Rearden says, "I know what they mean . . . your friendship and your oath by the only woman you ever—"

They all suddenly know what this means. Rearden steps forward and demands, "Is this the woman you love?" Looking at Dagny, Francisco answers, "Yes." Rearden slaps him across the face. Retaining iron control, Francisco bows and takes his leave.

Rearden suddenly wishes desperately that he hadn't reacted as he had. Dagny then reveals to Rearden that Francisco had been her first lover. In this private turmoil, they are interrupted by a message from Quentin Daniels: a letter of resignation. He refuses to continue working on the motor under Directive 10-289. Dagny phones him in Utah and begs him to meet with her first. Daniels gives his word that he'll wait for her visit.

When Rearden leaves, she summons Eddie to take instructions as she packs for the trip. Eddie notices a man's dressing gown in her closet bearing Hank Rearden's initials. Crushed with jealousy, Eddie realizes for the first time just how much Dagny has meant to him. That evening in the cafeteria he pours out his heart to his workman friend. He mentions that Dagny is on her way to try to talk Daniels out of quitting his work on the motor—and then blurts out his discovery that she is sleeping with Rearden. At this news, the worker seems unaccountably stricken and rushes out.

Dagny is racing by train across the country to her meeting with Daniels when she has a chance encounter with a hungry tramp. He explains that he once had been a machinist at the Twentieth Century Motor Company. One day the firm's heirs instituted a socialistic pay plan, based on the principle that everyone "would work according to his ability, but would be paid according to his need." In practice, this meant that workers of ability were punished with longer hours and forced to support "needier" workers—the lazy and incompetent—with compensation sufficient to fulfill all their alleged needs. Within months, everyone was hiding his abilities, but claiming a profusion of "needs"—and production plummeted until the factory went bankrupt.

The plan, the tramp continues, had been approved at a mass meeting of the workers. After the vote, a young engineer stood up. Speaking with moral confidence, he said he would "put an end to this" by stopping "the motor of the world." As the years passed, factories closed, and the economy ground to a halt, the tramp and his fellow workers wondered about the young engineer—and began to ask the despairing question now on everyone's lips. "You see," he tells Dagny, "his name was John Galt."

Dagny's journey is interrupted when the train's crew deserts at night in the middle of nowhere. She is surprised to see Owen Kellogg—the young man who had refused her job offer—riding the train, en route to a month-long vacation. Kellogg accompanies her up the track on foot to phone for help—and along the way, Dagny discovers that he too is part of the conspiracy. After arranging for help to come to the stalled train, she commandeers a small plane at a nearby airfield and flies alone to Utah to her meeting with Daniels. But upon arriving at the airport, she is told that Daniels has just left with another man, in a plane that has just taken off.

Determined not to lose Daniels to the "destroyer" spiriting him away, Dagny takes off again and races after the distant lights of the other plane. The long chase takes them over the wildest stretches of the Colorado Rockies. Unexpectedly, the stranger's plane begins to circle and descend over impossibly rugged mountain terrain, vanishing behind a ridge. When she reaches the spot, she sees nothing below but a rocky, inaccessible valley between granite walls: no conceivable place for a landing, yet no sign of the other plane. She descends but still sees nothing. Her altimeter shows her dropping—yet strangely, the valley floor seems to be getting no closer.

Suddenly there is a blinding flash of light, and her motor dies. Her plane spirals downward—not into jagged rocks, but toward a grassy field that hadn't existed a second before. Fighting to control the plane, she hears in her mind the hated phrase, not in despair, but this time in defiance: "Oh hell! Who is John Galt?"

PART THREE: A IS A

When she opens her eyes, Dagny is staring up at the proud, handsome face of a man with sun-streaked brown hair, and green eyes that bear no trace of pain, fear, or guilt. He reveals that he is John Galt.

Galt carries the injured woman away from the wreck. He explains that her plane had penetrated a screen of rays projecting a refracted image, like a mirage, intended to camouflage the valley's existence. The ray screen had killed her plane's engine.

He carries her past a small house, where the sound of a piano is lifting the chords of Halley's Fifth Concerto. It's Halley's home, Galt explains. They reach a ledge above the valley; a small town spreads below. Nearby, commanding the valley like a coat of arms, stands a solid gold dollar sign three feet high—"Francisco's private joke," he says.

A car pulls up, and its two occupants approach. She recognizes Hugh Akston. The other man is introduced as Midas Mulligan —the world's richest financier, who had also vanished years ago.

Smiling, Akston tells her that he never expected that when they next met, she would be in the arms of the inventor of the motor. Astounded, Dagny asks if the story of his walking out of the Twentieth Century Motor Company is true, and Galt confirms it. He has, he says, kept his promise to "stop the motor of the world."

Then he drives her around the valley, where she encounters others who have abandoned her world: Quentin Daniels . . . Dick McNamara, her former contractor . . . Ellis Wyatt . . . Ken Danagger . . .

Galt stops the car outside a lonely log cabin; above the door is the d'Anconia coat of arms. She gets out, staring at the silver crest, remembering the words of the man she had once loved. "That was the first man I took away from you," Galt says.

He ends the tour at the town's powerhouse, where his motor brings the valley its electricity. On it is an inscription: I SWEAR BY MY LIFE AND MY LOVE OF IT THAT I WILL NEVER LIVE FOR THE SAKE OF ANOTHER MAN, NOR ASK ANOTHER MAN TO LIVE FOR MINE. Galt explains that it's the oath taken by every person in the valley except Dagny. Recited aloud, the words are also the key to unlocking the door.

That night they attend dinner at Mulligan's home with several of the prominent men who had vanished from her world. Each explains his reasons for quitting. Galt explains that they are on strike against the morality of self-sacrifice and the disdain of mind, production, and wealth.

Dagny asks about his motor. For the sake of what it meant to him, he says, he had to be willing to abandon it—"just as you will have to be willing to let the rail of Taggart Transcontinental crumble and vanish."

Galt drives her back to his home, carries her to the guest room, and places her upon the bed. Each is intensely aware of the other's physical presence.

The next day Ragnar Danneskjöld visits. Galt and Ragnar worry about Francisco, unaccountably late for their customary month's vacation in the valley. Galt tells Dagny she must remain the entire month. She insists on earning her keep as Galt's cook and maid.

When Owen Kellogg arrives days later, he tells her that everyone, including Hank Rearden, now believes she crashed in the mountains, and search parties are looking for her wreckage. But the rules of the valley permit no communication with the outside world.

In her room one day, Dagny hears a familiar voice: Francisco's. He tells Galt sadly that he must leave again right away. She hears Galt answer that before he does, he should see the "scab" living in his guest room. Francisco laughs and opens her door.

In the next moment he is on his knees, holding her. But when he raises his head, his eyes are laughing. He tells her that he loves her, that it doesn't matter that she loves Rearden—only that she's alive and in a place where all things are possible. Recalling the night twelve years earlier when he had left her, he explains that Galt had spoken to Ragnar and himself that very day to recruit them to his strike. It was seeing Dagny, and foreseeing her hopeless struggle, that had convinced him to be the first to join the strike. He concludes by saying that he doesn't blame her for being in love with Rearden.

But now Dagny realizes that this is no longer true. In the days that follow, she and Galt endure the tension of an overwhelming but impossible attraction: between the woman consecrated to saving Taggart Transcontinental, and the man determined to destroy it.

At last comes the night when, in Midas Mulligan's home, the strikers ask her to decide either to join the strike or to return to the world. While she ponders, Mulligan asks Galt if he's decided whether to return to New York. Galt answers cryptically that he's not certain. Surprised, Mulligan warns in graphic detail what the coming social chaos will be like. When he says the Taggart Bridge will fall, Dagny cries out, "No, it won't!" She has decided to return.

Walking home that night, Francisco—who has been looking at Galt and Dagny thoughtfully—invites them for a drink at his cabin. He asks Galt casually if he's finally made up his mind whether to return to New York. Galt answers yes. Francisco looks at them both, understanding. From silver goblets of his Spanish ancestors, they share a toast that seals their mutual acceptance.

Galt and Dagny spend their last sleepless night in separate rooms of Galt's house. The next morning, after securing her promise of secrecy about the valley, Galt flies her, blindfolded, to a dying town and leaves her in a dying world . . .

. . . a world where Dr. Robert Stadler is summoned by Dr. Floyd Ferris to the first public demonstration of the State Science Institute's "Project X"—a secret invention of which Stadler knows nothing. The media and national figures are present, including Mr. Thompson, head of state. Ferris announces that Project X is a sonic ray device—"an invaluable instrument of public security" with a radius of a hundred miles. It is, he announces, a practical application of Stadler's own scientific theories: in fact, Stadler's ideas and reputation allowed the project to be planned and funded. The physicist and onlookers are horrified when, in the demonstration, the ray annihilates a distant farm. But when Ferris hands him a prepared speech to reassure the crowd, Stadler meekly obeys.

Dagny returns to a New York City close to collapse. She phones Hank, who is shocked with relief to hear her voice—but puzzled by her failure to answer questions as to where she has been, and why she hasn't communicated with him.

Eddie tells her that in her absence a Railroad Unification Plan—run by a thug named Cuffy Meigs—has socialized the nation's railroads. All must allow their competitors' trains to use their track without charge. Their revenues are pooled, and income comes in the form of government subsidies, based on miles of track, not traffic. Because Taggart has the most track, it is making money—and destroying its competitors.

Jim insists she go on the radio on the government's behalf, to reassure the nation that she hasn't quit. Dagny refuses. That evening she receives a surprise visit from Lillian. Rearden's wife reveals why he had signed the "Gift Certificates," and now tries to use the same blackmail over the affair to force Dagny to appear on the radio show. Dagny coolly agrees—then, on the air, proudly tells the world that she'd been Rearden's mistress for two years and publicly exposes the blackmail scheme.

She finds Rearden waiting back at her apartment. He confesses his love for her, and his liberation from guilt. He also tells her, serenely, what he has guessed: that during the month of her disappearance, she met the man she now loves—and that was the reason she had not contacted him. Dagny confirms that the "John Galt" of legend exists, that he is the inventor of the motor, and "the destroyer"—and also the man she loves.

James has been plotting with Latin American politicians to fleece the carcass of d'Anconia Copper, secretly scheduled for global nationalization on September 2. He feels the need to celebrate and returns home to his young wife, Cherryl. In the year of their marriage, she has learned that her husband isn't the man she had once imagined. She's visited Eddie, who has revealed the truth about who really runs Taggart Transcontinental. Now the need to justify himself compels James to boast to her of the forthcoming nationalization of d'Anconia Copper. Disgusted, Cherryl walks out. She visits Dagny and apologizes for her past insults. She explains that she now realizes her husband is motivated by a form of viciousness that she can't understand. Dagny is concerned: Cherryl seems terribly fragile.

At the same moment, James is visited by Lillian, who begs for help in stopping her pending divorce. "I don't want to let him go free!" she cries. "I won't let the whole of my life be a total failure!" They get drunk. Then, motivated by a mutual, blind desire to defile Rearden by means of his wife, they have sex.

Cherryl returns home and is shocked to hear a woman's voice in her husband's bedroom. After the woman leaves and she confronts James, he screams at her, boasting that it was "Mrs. Hank Rearden." When Cherryl asks why he'd married her, he yells that it was precisely because he'd seen her as worthless. She backs away, horrified. "You're a killer . . . for the sake of killing," she says.

Spirit shattered, she rushes from the apartment, wandering blankly through the neighborhood. When a social worker confronts and berates her, it is too much: Cherryl runs from the woman and plunges into a river to her death.

On the morning of September 2, the radio announces that just as the Chilean legislature met to nationalize d'Anconia Copper, explosions rocked the company's ore docks—and simultaneously, all d'Anconia Copper holdings around the world. The d'Anconia fortune is gone, as is its owner. James and his cronies, who had invested secretly in the cartel that was to take over the nationalized assets, have lost their investments.

That night, Dagny and Rearden meet at a restaurant. Suddenly there's a muffled scream. Beyond the window, an enormous calendar page on a building is changing. The date disappears—replaced by a huge, handwritten message:

BROTHER, YOU ASKED FOR IT!

Francisco Domingo Carlos Andres Sebastián d'Anconia

Amid the cries of alarm, Hank Rearden rises to his feet, laughing.

In the ensuing days, Dagny works to cope with daily emergencies stemming from the loss of copper. More businesses everywhere are closing their doors; supplies of all sorts of materials are drying up; and the nation faces the coming winter desperately short of fuel. But with every new crisis, the government finds new ways to make matters worse.

The government orders freight cars intended for the Minnesota wheat crop to be diverted to Louisiana for a soybean project run by the politically connected. The wheat harvest lies in heaps and is destroyed by rain. Bankrupted farmers begin to riot, and Minnesota plunges into primitive savagery.

When a copper wire breaks, all signals go down in the tunnels beneath the Taggart Terminal, and traffic is at a standstill. Dagny rushes to the terminal to take charge, still in a formal black dress from a dinner. From the stairway of the underground traffic tower, she organizes a large gang of laborers to man the tracks with lanterns and explains that they will guide trains in and out of the tunnels.

She stops. Among the upturned faces of the men, in greasy overalls and shirtsleeves, stands a man with sun-streaked copper hair and ruthlessly perceptive eyes. She finishes her instructions . . . then descends the stairs, making her way toward abandoned tunnels. He follows—and at last Dagny Taggart and John Galt consummate what had begun twelve years before.

Afterwards he tells her that for all those years he'd been working beneath her feet, as a common laborer in the tunnels. He warns her that their meeting would have bad consequences, because her goals would one day force her to lead his enemies to him.

Abruptly, the government provokes a series of outrageous actions against Rearden: fomenting violence at his plant, demanding raises for his workers, seizing his property on trumped-up tax charges. Rearden does not rise to the bait: he remains silent, refusing to respond or protest. Within days, he receives profuse apologies about "misunderstandings" and is invited to a meeting of high-level officials at the Wayne-Falkland Hotel on November 4.

That morning he receives a call from his mother, begging to see him that afternoon. When he arrives at his former home, he finds his mother, Philip—and Lillian: they'd been letting her live there secretly, at his expense. Rearden refuses their demands to do anything about the government's attachment of their allowance checks. His mother accuses him of not caring about them. "I don't," he answers. Eventually, she blurts out, "If you give up and vanish, like all those men who—"

Now he understands: even though his position is hopeless, and in reason his only course is to quit—they still want him to sacrifice the last of himself for their sakes. His mother screams that they want to live, but Rearden suddenly realizes they don't: if they had valued their lives, they would have valued him. As he turns to go, Lillian, her voice filled with malice, tells him that while still his wife, she had slept with Jim Taggart. It's meant to hurt him; but he looks at her with utter indifference. Before his eyes, Lillian's features slacken; her quest for power over him has met its final, irrevocable defeat.

Rearden drives to the New York hotel where Wesley Mouch, Jim Taggart, Floyd Ferris, and others await him. They beg for his agreement to a Steel Unification Plan, modeled after the Railroad Unification Plan. Each steel company will produce as much as it can, "according to its ability"; their gross earnings will be confiscated and placed in a common pool; then each company will be paid "according to its need." Since the preservation of blast furnaces is determined to be the "basic need," companies will be rewarded according to their number of furnaces.

By this scheme, Rearden would be paid for less than half his actual output, while Orren Boyle—having many idle furnaces—would be paid for nearly double his output. Rearden challenges them to explain how "to make the irrational work."

"Oh, you'll do something!" James Taggart cries.

Rearden suddenly grasps the nature of his enemies—and who has been empowering them. They were counting on him to buy them just a little more time, before he too would be destroyed. . . . He leaves them and drives back to Philadelphia, to his mills. A mile away he hears gunfire: a mob is trying to storm the main gate. Turning down a side road, he screeches to a stop and jumps out, half-sliding down the ravine to where he has spotted a human form.

It is Tony, the "Wet Nurse," mortally wounded. The boy tells him that the looters in Washington had planned to stage a phony riot of allegedly starving workers at his mills, to justify imposing the Steel Unification Plan. But Tony had refused to sign the passes to admit hired goons onto the property. When he ran for help, they shot him.

Rearden struggles to carry him out of the ravine, but Tony dies in his arms. He walks on, his rage growing, and leaves the boy's body in the infirmary. Then he heads for the front gate. To his surprise, there is organized resistance to the goons. On a roof he spots a man firing down at the rioters; the man sees him and abandons his post.

Then Rearden is confronted by two thugs. In the instant when they strike him with clubs, he hears a gun blast, and a strong arm breaks his fall as he collapses into darkness. . . .

He awakens in his office, the mill's doctor hovering over him. He asks who had saved his life. The doctor replies that it was Frankie, the new furnace foreman, who had learned of the plot and organized the defenses. Rearden asks to see him.

The door opens. Standing proudly, streaked with soot, is Francisco d'Anconia. Rearden acknowledges Francisco's friendship, and says he is ready to hear what his friend has to say.

The next morning, Dagny laughs triumphantly as James shrieks hysterically that Rearden has quit and vanished. The newspapers try to cover up the story as the nation slips into near-anarchy. They announce an upcoming radio address by Mr. Thompson on the world crisis, scheduled the night of November 22.

James tells Dagny that the head of state personally has invited her to confer with him at the studio before the broadcast. She arrives with Eddie Willers to find the whole Washington gang present; so is Robert Stadler. Just before eight o'clock, a technician rushes in with the news that all radio stations in the country have gone off the air simultaneously, their signals overwhelmed by waves of some unknown frequency and source. Mr. Thompson yells impotently for somebody to do something.

"Ladies and gentlemen," says a voice from a nearby radio, ". . . this is John Galt speaking."

In the three hours that follow, Galt tells the world about the strike and his reasons for it. He reveals the philosophical meaning and cause of the world's crisis—and the cure: "We are on strike against self-immolation. We are on strike against the creed of unearned rewards and unrewarded duties. We are on strike against the dogma that the pursuit of one's happiness is evil." Damning the ideas of mysticism, altruism, and collectivism, he outlines the basis for a new morality: a morality of rational self-interest. (See the third part of this book, "The Philosophy.")

When the speech ends, Mr. Thompson demands that somebody tell him what to do. Dagny tells him to give up power. Robert Stadler tells him not to listen. When she and Eddie leave in disgust, Stadler coldly says his former student must be killed. He suggests finding Galt by tracking Dagny. Thompson agrees to track Dagny, but not to kill Galt. He says they'll make a deal and get him to save them.

As violence begins to overwhelm the country, as more and more men of talent vanish each day, as fewer and fewer products appear in stores, as Rearden Steel is nationalized, then closed—news broadcasts implore John Galt to negotiate with Mr. Thompson. There is no response.

Mr. Thompson warns Dagny that the national leadership is divided into two factions: his own, which abhors violence, and the Ferris-Meigs faction, which is urging him to control the nation through a reign of terror. Casually, he wonders aloud if their goons may already have found and killed Galt. His ploy works.

Desperately anxious, Dagny looks up Galt's address on the Taggart payroll. Then she makes her way through a slum neighborhood to an ancient tenement and rings the doorbell. The door opens and John Galt stands before her. She collapses in his arms.

He warns her that she undoubtedly has been followed. If the government learns what they mean to each other, they'll torture her to force him to comply with their orders. So when police arrive, he tells her, she is to turn him in and claim the reward. Reluctantly, Dagny agrees. Then he shows her a locked room: inside is his scientific laboratory, its equipment powered by his motor.

When a group of soldiers arrives, Galt and Dagny begin their charade. She identifies him, and he feigns anger. He refuses to open his laboratory door, and the goons force the lock—only to find nothing inside but piles of dust.

They take Galt to the Wayne-Falkland Hotel, to create the illusion that he's not a prisoner, but armed guards are at his door. A series of visitors, beginning with Mr. Thompson, argue, beg, and threaten

Galt, trying to get him to tell them what to do to save their skins. Thompson even offers him Mouch's role as economic dictator of the nation. Galt replies that he'll follow any order at gunpoint; but he won't think for them. "When you force a man to act against his own choice and judgment, it's his thinking that you want him to suspend. You want him to become a robot. I shall comply."

The other officials fare no better; most dread the prospect of facing again the eyes that see too much, the voice that names what they wish to evade. And as factories continue to close, and rioting expands into regional insurrections, pollsters find that nobody believes government propaganda that Galt is cooperating with them.

Dagny receives a message from Francisco telling her to watch the officials closely and to call him when she thinks Galt needs help. The looters are at the end of their rope. Ferris suggests torture, which horrifies Mr. Thompson: he desperately doesn't want to believe that he's the thug Galt said he was.

Mr. Thompson asks Galt if there is anyone he wants to see, and he asks for Dr. Robert Stadler. His former teacher is ordered into Galt's hotel room. "I couldn't help it, John!" he cries. Galt remains silent, which drives Stadler into a soliloquy of apologies—then excuses—then self-righteous insults—and finally the declaration that Galt must be "destroyed." He stifles a scream as he realizes what he's said. He moans. Stadler's monologue, Galt replies, has covered every point he had wanted to make to his former teacher. Stadler runs from the room.

A few days later, Galt is ordered to put on formal dinner clothes. He's taken to the hotel ballroom by a man who presses a hidden gun into his ribs. They enter to the standing ovation of five hundred guests, and Galt is seated as the guest of honor, between Mr. Thompson and the goon. After dinner, television equipment rolls forward, and an announcer welcomes everyone to the inauguration of "the John Galt Plan." Speakers commend him for his genius as a planner, his practical know-how, his selfless leadership. Mr. Thompson declares that Galt is present of his own free will, motivated by love for mankind and a sense of duty. Then he introduces Galt.

Galt rises swiftly and leans to one side, exposing the goon's gun to the viewing world. Then, staring into the camera, he says: "Get the hell out of my way!"

Robert Stadler hears this on his car radio, en route to the Iowa site of Project X. After Galt summoned him, government officials had become suspicious of his loyalties; he had felt cornered . . . but then remembered Project X. It was his property, after all, the product of his ideas. He drives frantically, vaguely planning to take control of the weapon and use it to defend himself from the Washington savages.

By intimidation he blusters his way past the guards at the site, which has been taken over by Cuffy Meigs. He finds Meigs in the control room, drunk. They begin a shouting match dangerously near the instrument panel, and Stadler orders Meigs not to touch it. But Meigs won't obey, and when one of his supporters tries to stop him, it only angers him more. "I'll show you who's boss," Meigs roars, and yanks a lever.

A crash of sound lifts and shatters the building—and within a diameter of two hundred miles, cities and farmhouses collapse into rubble. On the periphery of the circle, at the Mississippi River, a train and half of the Taggart Bridge tumble into the water.

Back at the ballroom, Dagny—who was one of the guests—leaves the panicked crowd and finds Mr. Thompson and his associates huddled together. Ferris is saying that only "direct action" will work now—that his "Ferris Persuader" at the State Science Institute in New Hampshire can force Galt to comply. James is eager to try the device, and finally even Mouch and Thompson go along.

Dagny phones Francisco, then hurries to her apartment and to her office to pack. Suddenly her chief engineer rushes in with the news of the destruction of the Taggart Bridge. Gasping, she leaps to the phone . . . then lowers it slowly.

She leaves Taggart Transcontinental for the last time. Outside, she sees that news of the Project X disaster has pushed the city into chaos. Francisco approaches her, and facing him, she solemnly repeats the Striker's Oath. . . .

In the basement of a small concrete structure at the State Science Institute, John Galt lies naked, strapped to a mattress. Electrodes attached to his body lead to a machine whose control panel is manned by a young mechanic. Taggart, Mouch, and Ferris sit nearby. Ferris tells Galt, "We want ideas—or else." Galt remains silent. Ferris orders a series of electrical shocks sent through Galt's body. But he refuses to speak.

Suddenly the machine stops. The young mechanic stares at it with a look of incomprehension. Then they hear Galt's voice . . . instructing him on how to fix it.

Horrified, the mechanic runs from the room. "No!" James Taggart cries. Mouch tries to calm Taggart, but he won't have it. "I want to break him! I want to hear him scream. I want—" And then Taggart himself screams, realizing that he wants Galt to die even though it would cost his own life.

Taggart collapses. Shaken, Ferris and Mouch lead him from the room.

Dagny, Francisco, Ragnar, and Rearden invade the grounds of the State Science Institute. After overcoming the guards in brief gun skirmishes, they race downstairs to the cellar. They free Galt and lead him back to their plane.

Before long the glowing skyline of New York rises before them. In moments, they are looking down at the city. Suddenly the buildings seem to vanish; it takes a moment to realize that the lights of New York have gone out. . . .

On the Arizona desert, the train bearing Eddie Willers breaks down. The crew tries vainly to repair the engine. Then a line of covered wagons approaches. The leader tells Eddie that going on is useless: the Taggart Bridge to the East is now gone. The terrified passengers accept his offer to join his horse-drawn caravan. But Eddie refuses. "Don't let it go!" he cries, as they leave him in the darkness. Eddie steps to the front of the engine, looks up helplessly at the letters TT— then collapses across the rails, sobbing. . . .

It is an evening in the valley. The strikers are putting finishing touches on their future plans. On a high ridge above them, Galt and Dagny walk in the starlight. Then Galt stops, looking off into the distance beyond the mountains.

"The road is cleared," he says. "We are going back to the world."

ATLAS SHRUGGED TIMELINE

DAVID KELLEY

tlas Shrugged has a timeless quality that one finds in many epics. The narrative does not place the story at a specific point in real time—not by actual dates, nor by references to actual events such as World War II, nor by historically recognizable customs, fashions, technology, or the like. On the latter score, indeed, the novel achieves its timeless quality partly from the incongruous juxtaposition of elements. Railroads, for example, were already declining as a means of transportation when Rand wrote the novel, but there are also futuristic devices like Galt's motor and the Project X weapon based on Stadler's discoveries about cosmic rays. All we can say is that the story is set at an unspecified time in the future.

In a letter to a fan, Rand said

> You ask whether *Atlas Shrugged* represents the present or the future. The answer is: both. To be exact, the action of *Atlas Shrugged* takes

place in the near future, about ten years from
the time when one reads the book.

The time setting of the novel, in other words, is perpetually "the day after tomorrow," moving like the horizon to remain a constant distance ahead.

Nevertheless, the events of the novel are dated internally by month and season in a carefully plotted sequence. In the study of narrative, it is common to distinguish between plot time and story time. The former is the "present time" of the events and characters. *Atlas Shrugged* opens on September 2 of Year 1, and the plot time is three and a half years, ending in February or March of Year 5.

Story time, on the other hand, includes not only the present of the narrative but also the prior events that are mentioned or implied and that have brought the characters and the world to the point at which we first encounter them. *Atlas Shrugged* has the structure of a mystery or detective story. As in conventional stories of this type, the protagonists are trying to solve puzzles—an abandoned motor of revolutionary potential, the disappearance of top producers—that arose from events in the past. In addition, each of the characters has a history. Dagny is 34 when the novel opens; Francisco, Ragnar, and Galt are 36; Hank is 45. We learn a lot about their previous experiences, including the love affair between Dagny and Francisco, Hank's rise in the steel business and his marriage to Lillian, and of course the event that finally explains the puzzles: Galt's decision to launch his strike twelve years before Year 1.

Some writers have attempted to create timelines for the entire story time of the novel, putting relative dates on events in the backstory. That is a complex and somewhat speculative task; for those who are interested, I recommend Robert Bidinotto's "*Atlas Shrugged* Timeline."[1] But here we will just cover plot time, including the essential turning points from Year 1 to Year 5.

---

1   Robert Bidinotto, "Atlas Shrugged Timeline," http://www.atlassociety.org/atlas-shrugged/atlas-shrugged-timeline.

For most of them, we are given the month in which it occurred, and the timeline is organized accordingly. When we are given an exact date, I have included that as well.

Year 1

September

2   Eddie reports train wreck to Jim. Dagny tells Jim she is buying Rearden Metal rails. Owen Kellogg quits (I, 1).

Hank Rearden pours first heat of Rearden Metal (I, 2).

October

Mouch betrays Hank in deal with Jim and Orren Boyle (I, 3).

Dick McNamara disappears (I, 4).

Mexico nationalizes San Sebastián mines, which are found to be worthless (I, 4).

15   "Anti-Dog-Eat-Dog Rule" passes, Conway accedes, Dagny is given nine months to rebuild Rio Norte line; Wyatt issues threat (I, 4).

December

10   Reardens' anniversary party: Francisco meets Hank; Dagny trades with Lillian for Rearden Metal bracelet (I, 6).

Year 2

January

State Science Institute report attacks Rearden Metal (I, 7).

Dagny forms company to build John Galt Line (I, 7).

Equalization of Opportunity Bill passes, forcing Hank to sell businesses (I, 7).

February – June

Dagny builds Line to meet July deadline for shipping Wyatt oil (I, 7).

Dwight Sanders disappears (I, 7).

July

22   First run on the John Galt Line. Dagny and Rearden begin their affair (I, 8).

23   Jim meets Cherryl (I, 9).

August

Mouch becomes head of Bureau of Economic Planning (I, 9).

October – December

Dagny and Hank find motor in Starnes factory (I, 9).

Dagny meets Akston at his diner (I, 10).

Mouch issues directives affecting trains, metals (Fair Share Law), Colorado; Wyatt sets oil fields ablaze and disappears (I, 10).

Year 3

January

Stockton, Hammond disappear (II, 1).

March

Dagny consults Stadler about motor, hires Daniels to work on it (II, 1).

May

Rearden refuses to sell any Rearden Metal to State Science Institute (II, 1).

September

Rearden makes illegal deal with Danagger to sell Rearden Metal (II, 2).

2 Jim's and Cherryl's wedding: Francisco's "money speech" (II, 2).

Lillian discovers Hank is having an affair (II, 3).

October

Ferris threatens Hank with prosecution unless he supplies Rearden Metal to SSI; Hank refuses (II, 3).

Hank and Danagger indicted; Danagger disappears (II, 3).

November

Hank is acquitted at trial (II, 4).

Hank visits Francisco, tells of ordering copper. Ragnar sinks ship (II, 4).

Year 4

February

Atlantic Southern bridge collapses (II, 5).

15 Taggart directors decide to close John Galt Line (II, 5).

March

Ted Nielsen disappears (II, 5).

31 John Galt Line closes (II, 5).

April

2 Lillian meets with Jim to conspire against Hank, then discovers that Hank's affair is with Dagny (II, 5).

May

1 Directive 10-289 is issued; Dagny quits and goes to Berkshire cabin (II, 6).

15 Rearden signs rights to Rearden Metal over to government (II, 6).

27 Winston tunnel disaster (II, 7).

28 Dagny returns to office, then leaves to try to reach Daniels before he disappears (II, 8-9).

30 Dagny hears story of Galt leaving Starnes factory (II, 10).

31 Dagny crashes in valley (II, 10).

June

Dagny spends month in valley, leaves at end (III, 1-2).

29 Demonstration of Project X (III, 3).

July

Lillian tries blackmailing Dagny to support government; Dagny's speech reveals scheme (III, 3).

August

James, Boyle, et. al. make deal over nationalization of d'Anconia Copper (III, 4).

6 Cherryl commits suicide (III, 4).

September

2 Attempted nationalization of d'Anconia Copper fails (III, 5).

October

> Minnesota harvest disaster (III, 5).

> 15 Dagny sees Galt among track workers; they consummate affair (III, 5).

November

> 4 Attack on Hank's mills; Wet Nurse killed; Francisco saves Hank's life. Hank joins strike (III, 6).

> 22 Galt's speech (III, 7).

Year 5

January

> 22 Rearden's factory closes (III, 8).

February

> Dagny goes to Galt's apartment; Galt is captured (III, 8).

> Stadler and Meigs fight for control of Project X; Meigs blows them up, destroys Taggart Mississippi bridge (III, 9).

> Galt tortured. Dagny joins strike, helps rescue Galt. Strikers return to valley. Lights of NYC go out (III, 10).

CAST OF CHARACTERS

ALEXANDER R. COHEN
AND ROBERT BIDINOTTO

Ayn Rand wrote novels in order to depict her ideal man. Her crowning achievement in that regard is John Galt, the man who stops the motor of the world. But there are more than eighty characters, heroic and otherwise, in *Atlas Shrugged*. Some are outstanding men and women of the mind; some are evaders in jobs that require great thinkers. Some are thinkers and producers who work on a smaller scale; some are small-time moochers and looters. And while the main heroes (except John Galt!) are in business, there are both admirable and vicious characters in a variety of professions. Many of their stories illustrate, in different respects, how a person's thinking or refusal to think and the values he chooses shape his life, his character, and the world. In this list, we present all (we think!) of the characters to whom Rand gave at least partial names:

AKSTON, DR. HUGH. World-renowned philosopher, formerly head of the department of philosophy at Patrick Henry University in Cleveland. John Galt, Francisco d'Anconia, and Ragnar Danneskjöld are among his former students. He is persuaded to join their strike; as a striker, he flips hamburgers in a roadside diner in Wyoming and works for Mulligan Tobacco in Galt's Gulch.

ATWOOD, CALVIN. Owner of Atwood Light and Power Company. He joins the strike, becoming a shoemaker and owner of Atwood Leather Goods in Galt's Gulch.

BASCOM, MAYOR. Sleazy mayor of Rome, Wisconsin, who briefly owns the Twentieth Century Motor Company after the failure of Eugene Lawson's Community National Bank.

BEAL, LUKE. A Taggart fireman who is good at his job but not capable of anything more intellectually demanding. He is the only known survivor of the Taggart Tunnel disaster.

BLODGETT, DR. Keyboard operator of Project X.

BOYLE, ORREN. Head of Associated Steel and of the National Council of Metal Industries. Boyle conspires with James Taggart and the government to destroy his competitor, Hank Rearden, and seize the rights to produce Rearden Metal.

BRADFORD, LAURA. An actress trying to build her career by dating officials. Her final boyfriend, Kip Chalmers, likes her because she's Wesley Mouch's ex. She dies in the Taggart Tunnel disaster.

BRENT, BILL. Chief dispatcher of Taggart Transcontinental's Colorado division. He quits rather than carry out Dave Mitchum's order to send a coal-burning locomotive through the Taggart Tunnel.

CHALMERS, KIP. A bureaucrat turned politician. He pressures James Taggart to let his train run through a Colorado tunnel even though only a dangerous coal-burning locomotive is available. This leads to a major disaster.

CHALMERS, MA. A sociologist and converted Buddhist who gains prestige when her son Kip dies in the Taggart Tunnel. In an effort to make Americans more like "the peoples of the Orient," she backs a subsidized soybean project that fails.

COLBY, TOM. Leader of the Rearden Steel Workers Union; rolling mill foreman; the moral antithesis of Fred Kinnan. He and Rearden respect each other as allies, not adversaries.

CONWAY, DAN. President of the Phoenix-Durango Railroad. Conway is forced out of business in an industry conspiracy engineered by James Taggart and Orren Boyle.

DANAGGER, KEN. Founder of Danagger Coal. Danagger secretly buys Rearden Metal in violation of government regulations. While under indictment, he quits and joins Galt's strike.

D'ANCONIA, FRANCISCO. The spectacularly able president of d'Anconia Copper and Dagny Taggart's first lover, Francisco is the first man to join Galt's strike—and he gives up Dagny to do so. He adopts the guise of an international playboy as camouflage while he deliberately destroys his industrial empire over a period of years. Francisco is also one of the strike's recruiters, and his speeches on the moral meaning of money and on sex help to liberate Hank Rearden from guilt.

D'ANCONIA, SEBASTIÁN. Founder of d'Anconia Copper; the revered ancestor of Francisco d'Anconia.

DANIELS, QUENTIN. A talented young scientist who chooses to be a night watchman rather than serve the government. Dagny hires him to try to rebuild the motor she and Rearden discover at the abandoned Twentieth Century Motor Company. When he's recruited by Galt, Dagny follows their plane to Galt's Gulch.

DANNESKJÖLD, RAGNAR. College friend of Francisco and Galt; budding young philosopher. Ragnar is the third to go on strike. A man of implacable justice, he becomes a feared pirate who sinks government relief ships. He marries the beautiful actress Kay Ludlow.

EUBANK, BALPH. The proclaimed literary leader of the age—whose plotless novels don't sell. He decries commercialism and materialism.

FERRIS, DR. FLOYD. Top coordinator of State Science Institute, who works to harness science to serve the authorities. He blackmails Rearden into surrendering the patent rights to Rearden Metal. Later, Ferris urges the torture of John Galt with his machine, the "Ferris Persuader."

GALT, JOHN. The main hero of *Atlas Shrugged*, immortalized in the slang expression, "Who is John Galt?" John Galt is the man behind the two mysteries Dagny investigates: it is he who created the motor she discovers in the ruins of the Twentieth Century Motor Company's factory; and it is he who is persuading great achievers and ambitious producers to disappear from the world. Yet for much of the novel we see him only as Eddie Willers's nameless friend and confidant in the railroad's cafeteria. At the novel's climax Galt explains the philosophy behind the strike in a radio address. In "The Objectivist Ethics," Rand describes Galt as the "best representative" of her moral view.

GONZALES, RODRIGO. A Chilean diplomat who is said to have joined his country's government after it expropriated his property. He is involved in the attempt to seize d'Anconia Copper.

GONZALES, SEÑORA. Rodrigo Gonzales's wife. He trades her sexual favors.

HALLEY, RICHARD. A brilliant composer who achieves belated recognition after a long, grueling struggle. On his night of triumph, Halley retires and vanishes.

HAMMOND, LAWRENCE. Owner of Hammond Cars, maker of the nation's finest automobiles; another recruit to Galt's Gulch.

HARPER, POP. Taggart Transcontinental's aging, loyal chief clerk.

HASTINGS, WILLIAM. As chief engineer of the Twentieth Century Motor Company, John Galt's boss. He joins Galt's strike, but by the time the novel opens, he has been dead several years.

HASTINGS, MRS. The gracious, dignified widow of William Hastings. Dagny interviews her on the trail of the inventor of the motor.

HENDRICKS, DR. THOMAS. A renowned physician and medical researcher. He goes on strike when medicine is socialized.

HOLLOWAY, TINKY. An influential Washington bureaucrat allied to Orren Boyle and Wesley Mouch.

HUNSACKER, LEE. Ex-president of Amalgamated Service Corporation, which Dagny learns took over the bankrupt Twentieth Century Motor Company. His successful lawsuit against banker Midas Mulligan for not giving him a loan prompts Mulligan and Judge Narragansett to join the strike. Hunsacker is descended from members of the New York Four Hundred, and by the time Dagny meets him he's staying with friends for lack of a home of his own.

IVES, GWEN. Hank Rearden's loyal, supremely competent secretary.

KEITH-WORTHING, GILBERT. Elderly, has-been British author; friend of Kip Chalmers; advocate of collectivism. He dies in the Taggart Tunnel disaster.

KELLOGG, OWEN. Skilled young assistant to the manager of the Taggart Terminal. He resigns despite Dagny's efforts to persuade him to stay —and he won't say why or where he's going. While hunting for "the destroyer," Dagny meets him on a train and realizes that he's now one of "the destroyer's" men.

KINNAN, FRED. Leader of Amalgamated Labor of America. Kinnan is a corrupt power-seeker—but more bluntly honest than the rest of the Washington gang with whom he conspires. He respects Galt.

LARKIN, PAUL. Inept businessman; old friend of the Reardens. Larkin betrays Rearden in order to obtain political influence. When Rearden is forced to sell his ore mines, Larkin buys them with loans from Rearden and the government. He assures Rearden he'll supply him with ore, but he does not do so.

LAWSON, EUGENE. A bureaucrat; formerly the "banker with a heart," but thanks to his humanitarian lending—and especially a loan to Hunsacker's organization that left Lawson with the Twentieth Century Motor factory—his Community National Bank in Wisconsin no longer exists. Dagny interviews him on the trail of the inventor of the motor, but he thinks she's after political favors. He is seen smiling at the thought of mass starvation and at the decision to torture John Galt.

LIDDY, MORT. A composer of film scores—including one incorporating and degrading a theme by Richard Halley—and modern symphonies; an associate of Balph Eubank's.

LOCEY, CLIFTON. A crony of Jim Taggart's who informally replaces Dagny as operating vice president when she quits over Directive 10-289. Evading responsibility at every turn, he causes chaos—including the Taggart Tunnel disaster.

LOGAN, PAT. The engineer who wins the drawing to run the first train on the John Galt Line. He eventually quits, abandoning a train.

LUDLOW, KAY. A famous and beautiful actress who, rejecting the values being celebrated in movies, goes on strike and retires to Galt's Gulch. She becomes Ragnar Danneskjöld's wife.

MARSH, ROGER. Producer of electrical appliances in Colorado and cabbages in Galt's Gulch. Before joining the strike, he says he'd be chained to his desk to avoid quitting, but he quits anyway.

MARTINEZ, MARIO. Treasurer of the Interneighborly Amity and Development Corporation, which has a contract to manage industrial enterprises for Southern Hemisphere "People's States."

McKIM, RAY. Fireman who wins the drawing to work on the first train on the John Galt Line.

McNAMARA, DICK. A competent Cleveland contractor to Taggart Transcontinental. Dagny relies on him to build the John Galt Line—but he goes on strike.

MEIGS, CUFFY. Director of unification under the Railroad Unification Plan; a superstitious, anti-intellectual thug. When the economy nears collapse, he seizes control of the government's "Project X" weapon to establish himself as a local dictator. Drunk, Meigs accidentally causes an enormous explosion that devastates much of the Midwest, destroys the vital Taggart Bridge over the Mississippi River, and kills both himself and Robert Stadler.

MITCHUM, DAVE. Superintendent of Taggart Transcontinental's Colorado Division. Mitchum got his job only because he was Claude Slagenhop's brother-in-law. His decision to let a coal-burning locomotive pull Kip Chalmers' train into the Taggart Tunnel leads to disaster.

MORRISON, CLARENCE ("CHICK"). The government's "morale conditioner" and chief propagandist. He helps engineer a TV broadcast to show Galt to the nation; when it backfires, he resigns and flees.

MOUCH, WESLEY. A failure in the private sector; a success in Washington. Hired as Rearden's lobbyist, he betrays him in exchange for a high government job with the Bureau of Economic Planning and National Resources. A faceless nobody who constantly pleads for "wider powers," he is regarded as "safe"—and is promoted until he becomes the nation's economic dictator.

MOWEN, HORACE BUSSBY. Head of Amalgamated Switch and Signal Company. He initially resists agreeing to produce Rearden Metal switches for Taggart Transcontinental; then he agrees; then he decides to stop making them because it's unpopular. But once the

John Galt Line demonstrates what Rearden Metal can do, Mowen demands a law to give him a "fair share" of it. Mowen cannot understand why businesses are leaving more regulated states for less regulated ones.

MULLIGAN, MIDAS (NÉ MICHAEL). Brash, colorful owner of the Mulligan Bank of Chicago; early investor in Rearden Steel; the world's richest man. A humanitarian columnist dubbed him "Midas" as an insult; he changed his name. Mulligan goes on strike and vanishes when a court orders him to make a risky loan to Lee Hunsacker and his company to buy the Twentieth Century Motor Company factory. Mulligan then buys a remote valley in the Colorado Rockies, which he secretly develops as "Galt's Gulch."

NARRAGANSETT, JUDGE. Eminent legal scholar; judge on the Illinois Superior Court. Judge Narragansett goes on strike after his decision against Hunsacker is overturned by a higher court. He is designated the arbiter of disputes in Galt's Gulch, where he also owns a chicken and dairy farm.

NEALY, BEN. Contractor who takes over construction of the John Galt Line when McNamara quits. He is hostile and resentful of Dagny's demands for competent work.

NIELSEN, TED. Motor manufacturer in Colorado and an investor in the John Galt Line. Nielsen goes on strike when the line is shut down; he moves to Galt's Gulch, where he becomes a lumberjack.

POPE, BETTY. A slovenly society girl and James Taggart's mistress.

POTTER, DR. Lackey of Floyd Ferris at the State Science Institute who tries to coerce Rearden into selling Rearden Metal to the government.

PRITCHETT, DR. SIMON. Head of the philosophy department at Patrick Henry University after Hugh Akston's departure. A sophist who derides the power of reason, he's a valued intellectual excuse-maker for the Washington gang.

REARDEN, HENRY ("HANK"). Iron-willed inventor of Rearden Metal; founder of the Rearden Steel empire; one of the novel's three major heroes. Rearden's quest to understand and resolve his moral and emotional conflicts is central to the plot. His success makes him a target of predators in government, industry, and his own family. He becomes Dagny's secret lover and, to protect her reputation, surrenders the rights to Rearden Metal to the government in a blackmail scheme hatched by his wife. Rearden ultimately is rescued, physically and spiritually, by Francisco d'Anconia.

REARDEN, LILLIAN. Hank Rearden's wife. He marries her thinking she admires him, but she attempts to destroy his self-esteem. She is unwilling to divorce him even once she knows he is having an affair with Dagny. A friend of James Taggart's and a supporter of the Washington gang, she is the source of the secret information that is used as blackmail against Rearden in order to deprive him of Rearden Metal.

REARDEN, MRS. Rearden's petulant and parasitical mother, who berates him for the very achievements and virtues that maintain her comfortable lifestyle.

REARDEN, PHILIP. Hank's purposeless younger brother. Philip criticizes Hank's "materialism" and professes motivations "higher" than moneymaking, but that doesn't stop him from living off Hank's wealth—or betraying him.

SANDERS, DWIGHT. Owner of Sanders Aircraft, maker of the finest planes available. He sells that company to his brother so he can buy United Locomotive without breaking the law. Then he vanishes to Galt's Gulch and raises hogs.

SCOTT, JOE. A drunk who keeps his union job as a railroad engineer only because of his friendship with Fred Kinnan. He is at the throttle of the Comet, intoxicated, during its fateful trip into the Taggart Tunnel.

SCUDDER, BERTRAM. Editor of a left-wing rag, *The Future*; author of a scathing article about Hank Rearden titled "The Octopus"; foe of freedom, wealth, and industrialists. Dagny is blackmailed into appearing on his radio program, and after she reveals on the air that Rearden was blackmailed into signing over Rearden Metal and she was blackmailed into appearing on Scudder's program, Scudder is blamed and taken off the air—even though he says he was ordered to have her on his broadcast.

SLAGENHOP, CLAUDE. Pal of Philip Rearden; brother-in-law of Dave Mitchum; head of Friends of Global Progress, a militant and influential socialist group.

STADLER, DR. ROBERT. The world's greatest physicist; formerly head of the physics department at Patrick Henry University. But he believes reason and a commitment to truth are for "pure science"; in technology and politics, he thinks other standards apply. When Stadler endorses the foundation of the State Science Institute, Galt, until then his student, condemns him and quits his graduate program. Stadler becomes the Institute's titular head, lending his prestige to the organization and focusing on "pure theory," while Floyd Ferris runs the "practical" side, which uses Stadler's science to create the deadly weapon "Project X." By the end, Stadler discovers he wants Galt, the student he once loved, murdered. Stadler dies in the "Project X" explosion.

STARNES, ERIC. Youngest of the three worthless heirs of Twentieth Century Motor Company founder Jed Starnes; director of public relations under the heirs' collectivist scheme. He avenges himself on a girl who had rejected him, killing himself in her bedroom on her wedding day.

STARNES, GERALD. Heir, with his siblings, to the Twentieth Century Motor Company; director of production there under the heirs' collectivist scheme. While it lasts, he enjoys great wealth he claims is for everyone at the company; after it fails, he winds up a bum in a flophouse.

STARNES, IVY. Director of distribution at the Twentieth Century Motor Company. Of the three Starnes heirs, Ivy is the only one so committed to their collectivist ideals that she lives on the income of a typical worker. She relishes giving as little as she can to those who don't adequately kowtow. Blaming human nature for the failure of her and her siblings' scheme to run the company on the principle "from each according to his ability, to each according to his need," she turns for solace to Eastern mystical cults that disdain the physical world.

TAGGART, CHERRYL (NÉE BROOKS). An unsophisticated shop clerk who, believing him to be a great man on the basis of publicity that credits him with creating the John Galt Line, marries James Taggart and tries to live up to the role of his wife. But then she discovers the horrifying truth about his character and chooses to die rather than live on his terms.

TAGGART, DAGNY. Vice president in charge of operations and large stockholder, Taggart Transcontinental; descendant of railroad founder Nat Taggart; the novel's indomitable heroine and main viewpoint character. She struggles to save her business from government coercion and from the irrationality of her brother James, the company president. Despite such interference, she builds the John Galt Line from track made of Rearden Metal. Dagny struggles to discover the motives and identities of what seem to be two mysterious men: one, a "destroyer" who is deliberately draining the world of its most capable producers; the other, the inventor of the revolutionary motor whose remnants she has discovered in the ruins of the Twentieth Century Motor Company. She hires Quentin Daniels to try to reconstruct the motor. Then, when the hated "destroyer" recruits him, too, she pursues them by plane and crash-lands in Galt's Gulch. There she discovers that the "destroyer" and the inventor are the same man— John Galt—and she finds herself falling in love with her enemy. She is the last to join the strike.

TAGGART, JAMES. Dagny's older brother; president of Taggart Transcontinental; a major villain of the novel. James thwarts Dagny's every effort to salvage the railroad, and he uses his government connections to destroy his competitors. His power, reputation, wealth, and even survival are maintained only by Dagny's heroic efforts to save their company. He marries an innocent shop girl, Cherryl, to whom he is attracted by her misled admiration, but becomes enraged when she begins to see through him. At the story's end, his psychological destruction comes when he grasps that he wants Galt killed even though he knows it would mean his own death.

TAGGART, MRS. Mother of Dagny and James; host for a month each summer to the young Francisco. She is disappointed in her daughter's apparent lack of interest in beauty and romance.

TAGGART, NATHANIEL ("NAT"). The nineteenth-century founder of Taggart Transcontinental, revered by Dagny. His statue in the heart of the Taggart Terminal is a kind of spiritual shrine for her, and his courage and vision help to inspire her desperate desire to save the railroad.

THOMPSON, MR. "Head of the State"—not "president"—and a crafty pragmatist who believes everyone is open to compromise. His appearance is so unremarkable he's hard to identify. He tries to hire Galt as economic dictator, but he fails as Galt points out Thompson has no value to offer him. Eventually he reluctantly authorizes Galt's torture.

TUCK, LESTER. Campaign manager for Kip Chalmers. He dies in the Taggart Tunnel.

WARD, MR. Hard-working president of Ward Harvester Company who tries to keep his family business going by dealing with Rearden Steel.

WEATHERBY, CLEM. A bureaucrat lieutenant of Wesley Mouch with a candid, easy manner. He becomes Dagny's conduit in dealing with Washington.

WET NURSE, THE. Deputy Director of Distribution assigned to Rearden Metal. He goes from finding Rearden "impractical" to asking him for a productive job. When the government launches a violent attack on Rearden's mills, he gets wind of it and tries to stop the thugs. Only as he is dying do we learn his name is Tony.

WILLERS, EDDIE. Dagny's indispensable special assistant—a man of great integrity but modest ability, loyal to Dagny since childhood. Eddie frequently talks with a low-ranking Taggart employee whom he meets in the cafeteria and who becomes his private sounding board about Dagny and the railroad's problems. Eddie doesn't discover until too late that he loves Dagny—and that his attentive companion is John Galt.

WYATT, ELLIS. Head of Wyatt Oil, which he has grown from the barely profitable company his father ran into a pillar of the economy; inventor of a new method of extracting oil from rock. Wyatt becomes a friend of Dagny and Rearden. But when the government imposes a tax on Colorado that will bleed his business dry, he torches his oilfields in rebellion and joins the strike. One well fire can't be quenched. It becomes a symbol of the strike, known as "Wyatt's Torch."

ATLAS SHRUGGED
AS LITERATURE

ROBERT BIDINOTTO

One day in the 1940s, a young reporter asked Ayn Rand about the new novel he heard that she was planning. She replied: "It will combine metaphysics, morality, economics, politics, and sex—and it will show the tie between metaphysics and economics."

"I can't see how you'll manage it," the astonished reporter replied. "But I guess you know what you're doing."[1]

She certainly did. In the form of a suspenseful, romantic, tightly woven mystery spanning more than a thousand pages, and following scores of characters across a sweeping panorama of American life, Ayn Rand also dramatized and demonstrated every major aspect of a new moral code.

Literary scholar Kirsti Minsaas points out that Rand "uses the simple formula of a detective story to create a highly complex philo-

---

1   Barbara Branden, *The Passion of Ayn Rand* (Garden City, NY: Doubleday & Company 1986).

sophical novel, a novel where ideas are presented as answers to para-
doxical mysteries."[2]

Like a good symphony, *Atlas Shrugged* has many artistic riches
that become obvious only when we pay close attention, and after many
exposures. Its opening pages provide a perfect illustration.

As Eddie Willers walks the shabby streets of Manhattan, he
thinks of a huge oak tree of his childhood. It had been a symbol to
him of eternal strength. It would always be there, he had thought—
until the night the tree was struck by lightning and split in two. The
next day, standing before the fallen tree, Eddie was shocked to see that

> the trunk was only an empty shell; its heart
> had rotted away long ago; there was nothing
> inside—just a thin gray dust that was being
> dispersed by the whim of the faintest wind.
> The living power had gone, and the shape it
> left had not been able to stand without it.

Moments later, Eddie approaches the reassuring tower of Taggart Transcontinental, his mature symbol of enduring power and
strength, and he thinks of the company's proud slogan:

> From Ocean to Ocean, forever—thought
> Eddie Willers, in the manner of a rededica-
> tion, as he walked through the spotless halls
> into the heart of the building, into the office
> of James Taggart, President of Taggart
> Transcontinental.

It's clear that these passages are meant to serve several purposes. It's perfectly natural that the decaying city around him might
remind Eddie of the decayed oak tree of his childhood. The flashback
helps us understand his uneasy mood.

---

2   Kirsti Minsaas, "Structural Integration in Ayn Rand's *The Fountainhead* and *Atlas
    Shrugged*," in *The Literary Art of Ayn Rand*, ed. William Thomas (Poughkeepsie,
    NY: The Objectivist Center, 2005).

But Rand also intends the description of the tree's rotted trunk as a metaphor for Taggart Transcontinental. One clue is in her repetition of the word "heart." Just as the tree's "heart had rotted away long ago," so too had "the heart" of the Taggart Building, in the person of the company president. For there wasn't really anything inside James Taggart's office, either—just a graying, purposeless man who, like the dust inside the tree, was dispersed by the whim of any passing wind. Taggart Transcontinental's living power had also gone, and what was left couldn't continue to stand much longer.

Furthermore, the passage also stands as a metaphor for the whole crumbling culture—and the gray, dusty philosophy at its heart. It subtly and symbolically foreshadows the entire plot of the book.

Such symbolism is everywhere apparent in *Atlas Shrugged*, lending unusual emotional force to the ordinary details of scenes and events. Ayn Rand constantly places otherwise insignificant "concretes"—names, titles of chapters, events, objects of all sorts—into contexts which impress upon them a host of meanings and create a colorful tapestry of metaphor.

Take the chapter titled "The Top and the Bottom." It opens in an expensive rooftop restaurant that's low and dark, like a cellar. Inside, James Taggart and his powerful friends are conspiring to destroy their competitors. The chapter ends in the basement cafeteria of Taggart Transcontinental, a cheery place of space and bright light. Inside, Eddie Willers is chatting with a nameless railroad worker. Only much later in the novel does the reader realize that the anonymous worker is John Galt.

Ayn Rand is presenting a metaphor for the moral inversion of a corrupt society—for what happens in a society that rewards evil and punishes good. The chapter's title, and the events it depicts, illustrate what Minsaas describes as a "recurrent idea in Rand's novels[:] that in an irrational society, the best are frequently demoted to the bottom while the worst are to be found at the top."

Rand's subtlety extends to dialogue, too, where double and even triple meanings are often embedded in what seems to be casual conversation. For example, there are delightful ironies in many of the early references to John Galt, but since they occur before he appears in the story, most of them won't be apparent during a first reading.

When Dagny and Rearden discover Galt's abandoned motor, they ponder the fate of its unknown inventor. Rearden is certain that the man must be dead. If a mind that brilliant were still alive, he tells Dagny, "the whole world would know his name by now." A few moments later, he adds, wistfully, "*There* was the motor for the John Galt Line."

We can imagine the fun Ayn Rand must have had writing such lines.

Then there's the verbatim repetition, at the end of the story, of a passage that appears near its beginning: the description of the sounds of Halley's Fifth Piano Concerto.

> It was a symphony of triumph. The notes flowed up, they spoke of rising and they were the rising itself, they were the essence and the form of upward motion, they seemed to embody every human act and thought that had ascent as its motive. It was a sunburst of sound, breaking out of hiding and spreading open. ... Only a faint echo within the sounds spoke of that from which the music had escaped, but spoke in laughing astonishment at the discovery that there was no ugliness or pain, and there never had had to be. It was the song of an immense deliverance.

That description first introduces us to Dagny Taggart, capturing her idealistic yearnings. But when it's repeated at the end of the novel, the same description conveys a totally new meaning: not Dagny's longing for the ideal, but her triumphant achievement of it. Here, it gives us the satisfying feeling of a completed circuit—of an emotional benediction on her odyssey and our own.

But beyond such literary devices, Ayn Rand's most impressive talent is her power to integrate the novel's ideas with its plot elements.

One of the finest examples is in the passage describing the first run of the John Galt Line. Here, Ayn Rand connects the ironic symbolism of John Galt's name, the celebration of a great human achievement, the physical sensations of a train speeding across rails built of Rearden Metal, Dagny's realization about how the human mind gives spiritual meaning to physical matter—and the culmination of the growing romantic attraction between her and Rearden.

Consider the moment when Dagny enters the engine room of the locomotive. Staring at the engines, she realizes that they are a magnificent embodiment of human rationality. The motors, she thinks, are "a moral code cast in steel."

When she looks up, she sees Hank Rearden—the steel titan, the engine of the economy, the living embodiment of the rational creativity she worships—and their eyes meet across a space filled with the pounding rhythms of the train's motors.

To transform ideas of such abstract philosophical complexity into a passage of startling sensuality is a striking illustration of Rand's view that there should be no split between mind and body—between ideas and action. She saw human products as physical manifestations of man's spirituality—of his consciousness in action. And in this remarkable passage, she not only expresses that view philosophically: she illustrates it artistically, as well.

Like her philosophy, Ayn Rand's literary method challenges reigning orthodoxies. Bucking Naturalistic conventions, in which novelists try to copy all the mundane details of real life with absolute fidelity, Rand instead selected the details in her stories by reference to a single unifying idea. Here she was simply applying timeless rules of good dramatization.

In his celebrated classic, *The Art of Dramatic Writing*, literary instructor Lajos Egri points out that in a good story, everything is tightly integrated by some overarching theme or premise. The theme is the point or message that gives meaning to the story and that motivates the characters to act.

In an integrated story, no event, character, line of dialogue, or description is tossed in arbitrarily, simply because it sounds clever or interesting. According to Egri, everything must relate to the theme or premise. Indeed, "in a well-constructed play or story, it is impossible to denote just where premise ends and story or character begins."

Good drama is built on conflict. But as Egri says, "A weak character cannot carry the burden of protracted conflict in a play." Strong conflict requires extremely willful characters pursuing incompatible goals related to the story's theme. Their conflicts build powerfully throughout the story, until they're finally resolved in a climax that proves the story's theme. As Egri puts it: "Go through all great dramas and you will find that the characters in them *force the issue* in question until they are beaten or reach their goal."

Ayn Rand shared this view of good fiction writing. In *Atlas Shrugged*, her theme is the importance of reason to human life. So her plot, characters, dialogue, and descriptions all reinforce and advance that theme. Conflicts among and even within the characters are based on that theme, too; and the climax of the story—with mindless brutes desperately trying to force John Galt to think for them—finally demonstrates her theme. It proves not only why reason is important to human life, but why personal freedom is essential to reason.

Rand rejected the literary convention that "depth" and "plausibility" demand characters that are replicas of the kinds of people we meet in everyday life, uttering everyday dialogue and pursuing everyday values. But she also rejected the notion that characters should be symbolic rather than realistic.

"My characters are never symbols; they are merely men in sharper focus than the audience can see with unaided sight," she wrote to her agent Alan Collins. To a fan, she explained, "My characters are persons in whom certain human attributes are focused more sharply and consistently than in average human beings."

In other words, Rand stylized her characters. She focused selectively on the traits and motives that made each one distinctive, and eliminated the irrelevant or trivial aspects of their personalities or lives. What determined which traits and motives were essential? Her story's theme. Rand's characters are people seen through the filter of a guiding theme.

Take her opening description of Hank Rearden. She wished to portray him as a man of iron will and implacable self-discipline. She conveyed these qualities simply by the details she selected to describe his face while he watched Rearden Metal being poured from a blast furnace:

> The glare cut a moment's wedge across his eyes, which had the color and quality of pale blue ice—then across the black web of the metal column and the ash-blond strands of his hair—then across the belt of his trench-coat and the pockets where he held his hands. His body was tall and gaunt; he had always been too tall for those around him. His face was cut by prominent cheekbones and by a few sharp lines; they were not the lines of age, he had always had them: this had made him look old at twenty, and young now, at forty-five. Ever since he could remember, he had been told that his face was ugly, because it was unyielding, and cruel, because it was expressionless. It remained expressionless now, as he looked at the metal.

By eliminating accidental and superficial aspects of a character's personality, we can understand him much more deeply. Random details—such as Hank Rearden's favorite foods or flashbacks about his daily routines—would only divert our attention from his essential motives and purposes. Such trivia certainly wouldn't enhance, flesh out, or deepen our understanding of Rearden. They would only confuse us, making us wonder if these petty details were important to the author—or to Rearden himself. Their inclusion would make the drama diffuse, and blur the point of the story.

Another way to appreciate Rand's approach is to contrast it with that of other writers. The great Russian writer Dostoyevsky was also a master of dramatizing abstract philosophical and psychological themes. In his novel *The Possessed*, for example, he creates rich, highly detailed, and fascinating portraits of vicious, nihilistic characters. However, the sheer volume of such detail can be confusing; it suggests complex and competing motives at work in each character, and oftentimes it isn't easy to single out the most relevant of these.

By contrast, the more stylized portraits of evil characters in *Atlas Shrugged* don't offer as much psychological variety as those in *The Possessed*—or even as much variety as those Rand provides in her earlier masterpiece, *The Fountainhead*. That book explored many variations on the theme of psychological dependency. But in *Atlas Shrugged*, what Rand loses in diversity and complexity, she gains in depth and clarity. We get to probe the dominant motives of three major villains—Robert Stadler, Lillian Rearden, and James Taggart—down to their very roots. By the end of the novel, we have a much clearer and deeper insight into the minds of the moral traitor, the empty power-seeker, and the envious nihilist.

We also gain a greater grasp of the relationship between philosophical ideas and psychological states. Dostoyevsky shows us that such a link exists; Rand shows us how.

Probably the most criticized portions of *Atlas Shrugged* are the lengthy philosophical speeches made by her characters—especially Francisco's seemingly impromptu talk at a party on the moral meaning of money, and John Galt's climactic three-hour radio address. But these speeches weren't tacked onto the story for mere didactic purposes; rather, they're integrated parts of the plot, intended to propel the story forward.

Francisco's money speech, for instance, is meant to address Rearden's moral confusions and to liberate him from guilt. And it works: Francisco's words help Rearden to defend himself later at his trial; they foreshadow for him the rationale for the strike; and they move Rearden closer to fully grasping what is wrong with the world and to joining the strikers.

John Galt's long speech is actually the most decisive event in the plot. It moves all the events of the story toward the climax, forcing each character to take a final stand; it brings Dagny to the brink of understanding the nature of her enemies; it ties together all the key ideas previously presented in the story; and most importantly, it leads to Galt's capture by the fascist gang, which brings the story to its resolution. If he hadn't made the speech, the villains wouldn't even have known of his existence. As a result, the destruction of the country would have dragged out more slowly, and—from a literary standpoint—far less dramatically.

It's easy to see why *Atlas Shrugged* is almost impossible to categorize. Ayn Rand pushed the traditional boundaries of the novel form. How do you classify a book that offers a sixty-page discussion of metaphysics, ethics, and political economy—yet simultaneously contains such plot devices as a deadly ray device right out of science fiction, a philosopher-turned-pirate, a beautiful woman who falls in love with the man she's sworn to kill, and a finalé in which the hero is put onto a torture machine?

No wonder that Rand affectionately referred to *Atlas Shrugged* as her "stunt novel."[3] But her genius is that somehow, she made the stunt work. By any measure, *Atlas Shrugged* stands as one of the most remarkable and memorable feats of integration in the history of literature.

---

3   Nathaniel Branden, "The Literary Method of Ayn Rand," in *Literary Art*.

THE FILMS

John Aglialoro and Joan Carter at The Strike *premiere, October 2012*

THE HISTORY OF THE ATLAS SHRUGGED MOVIE TRILOGY

JOAN CARTER

This project began as I was cleaning out files. John Aglialoro is both my husband and my business partner so many of our files are co-mingled. John is a really good saver. Some people save everything—which means they really save nothing. I am not a saver at all, so things that I wish I could put my hands on are often long gone to the trash can. John saves judiciously. Not everything and not nothing—so what he has retained about the long journey to produce *Atlas Shrugged* is not a complete history, but selected highlights.

When I started to review the documents in his files, it was like a walk back through time and a rekindling of my admiration for the incredible tenacity it required to finally get the movie on the screen. It occurred to me that the effort should be documented—that sometime in the future someone might find inspiration in what he accomplished. So I began writing this history with only that in mind.

Obviously, some things have been omitted—things that are his private correspondences that I did not feel should be shared. The myriad legal documents that accompanied every transaction are also not included. But I have tried to capture the events I thought were most interesting to the vast number of people who have been out there rooting for him.

John would be the first to say that he did not do it alone—many individuals, named and unnamed, were important to the ultimate result. But, at the end of the day, one man—John Aglialoro—was responsible for bringing Ayn Rand's signature work, *Atlas Shrugged*, to the screens of America. This is how it happened.

THE EARLY YEARS OF OBJECTIVISM

John Aglialoro first read *Atlas Shrugged* in the summer of 1972, when he was 28 years old. Its message changed his life, much as it has changed the lives of millions of people who have read the epic novel. Twenty years later, in November 1992, Aglialoro purchased the rights to make the book into a movie—and thus began the history of the *Atlas Shrugged* movie trilogy.

The rights were purchased from Leonard Peikoff, Ayn Rand's legal heir. Aglialoro first became aware of Peikoff when he received a January 1985 letter in which Peikoff stated: "What is needed now, I believe, is a formal, centrally organized, highly visible structure through which to disseminate Objectivism to a much wider audience. That structure is the Ayn Rand Institute."

Providing the idea and the wherewithal to fund the Ayn Rand Institute (ARI) was Ed Snider, a businessman who had known Ayn Rand and believed that Rand's powerful message of individualism and the morality of capitalism had the potential to change lives. Snider knew that spreading the message was going to take a focused effort and it was going to take money. As Aglialoro often comments, if there is one individual who kept Objectivism alive through some pretty dark times, it is Ed Snider.

The first *ARI Newsletter* was published in December of 1985—Volume 1, No 1.

It contained a profile of Snider as well as the institute's announcement of the appointment of the first research fellow—none other than Dr. David Kelley, BA from Brown University and PhD in philosophy from Princeton.

(Kelley would later be asked to leave the institute when philosophical differences emerged between him and Peikoff and would go on to found what is today The Atlas Society.)

In September 1986, the Ayn Rand Institute's third *Newsletter* published an interview of Aglialoro in which he told the story of how the money speech in *Atlas Shrugged* gave him the moral basis for what he had always believed intuitively: that it is OK—not just OK, but critical to human happiness—to be an individual who lives for his own sake.

In May 1989, Aglialoro joined the institute's advisory board along with Judith Berliner, biologist and wife of Mike Berliner (ARI's executive director), and Richard Salsman, a commercial banker.

The year 1989 was eventful for the Objectivist movement. In a letter of April 21, 1989, Leonard Peikoff resigned from the ARI board citing the need to devote more time to his writing. And in December, Ed Snider resigned from the organization he had founded.

In addition to the additions and subtractions to the board, 1989 was the year in which Kelley was declared persona non grata based on his short essay, "A Question of Sanction," that took issue with an ARI position that true Objectivists do not speak with people with whom they disagree (in this case, libertarians). Kelley urged Objectivists to engage with adherents of other positions, from whom they might gain insights that enrich their own philosophy. Peikoff fired back with an article called "Fact and Value," which maintained that Objectivism is a completed system of ideas, not open to expansion, and asked those who are not in concert with him to leave the movement. The outcome of the philosophical dispute was a June 1, 1989, letter to Kelley from Michael Berliner. Berliner stated that Peikoff had conditioned the institute's continued use of the Ayn Rand name on the removal of Kelley from the institute and its speakers bureau. Berliner expressed his regret—but said Kelley had to go. The next year, Kelley founded the Institute for Objectivist Studies (now The Atlas Society) to promote Objectivism in a more open spirit.

During the years Aglialoro served on the ARI board, there were not only philosophical disagreements but organizational issues as well. Dr. Edwin Locke, a professor of business at the University of Maryland and ARI advisory board member, wrote to his fellow board members expressing Locke's concern about ARI governance. He wrote in August of 1993 that the board of directors of the institute was comprised of only two members (Harry Binswanger and Peter Schwartz). Further, Locke stated that the board of advisors was an under-used asset ("names on the stationery" rather than true advisors to the organization). This caused some furor.

Although Aglialoro did not feel qualified to comment on the philosophical arguments, he did respond to Locke with a letter giving his advice on proper organizational structure. He was vocal in his views that the institute should be governed like most corporate and even not-for-profit entities in America. He suggested that the advisory board be disbanded and its members made part of the board of directors, which should number 8-10 (or certainly not two). He also suggested that a primary function of a board is to provide succession. With Peikoff no longer part of the institute's governance, Aglialoro stated that the board should be tasked to consider future leadership of the organization.

Although he contributed time and money to the institute, Aglialoro's primary goal at the time was building his own business. He regarded the bickering at ARI as growing pains and tried to remain uninvolved in the types of arguments that often arise when individuals have strongly held but divergent views. His main objective was to get the ideas of Ayn Rand out into the world.

During the next few years, at every opportunity, Aglialoro voiced his belief that spreading the *Atlas Shrugged* message through college courses and essay contests was important, but that the most effective way to spread Rand's ideas to average Americans was to make *Atlas Shrugged* into a movie. He reiterated in many conversations with Peikoff that "the number of individuals who will watch a movie is far more than the number who will read an 1100 page book."

Peikoff also wanted to see the movie made and was not oblivious to the fact that, as the owner and proprietor of the movie rights, he stood to profit from a sale. There had been several prior attempts to make *Atlas Shrugged* into a movie, but, for a variety of reasons, it hadn't happened. Ed Snider had undertaken one such project to produce the movie, which, ultimately, he was forced to abandon.

Another effort to produce a film adaptation was put forward by Henry and Michael Jaffe. The major impediment was noted by Peikoff in a letter accompanying the Jaffe offering circular seeking investors for script development. While stating that the Jaffe organization would have the full support of both Peikoff and the Estate of Ayn Rand, he noted that previous efforts had been stymied "partly on ideological grounds and partly because [conventional sources of movie financing] objected to the author's estate having script approval."

Undaunted by prior misfires, Aglialoro continued to press Peikoff into trying to move *Atlas Shrugged* from book to screen. In August of 1992, they met in Aglialoro's home in Avalon, New Jersey, and struck a deal. Although the original handshake was for an outright sale transaction, the final agreement provided Aglialoro with 15 years to get the movie into principal photography. At the time, Aglialoro thought this would be no problem.

ATLAS FILM PRODUCTIONS AND THE SEARCH FOR A SCREENPLAY

To begin the process, Atlas Film Productions was formed, and Aglialoro's first mission was to raise money to fund production of the movie. In March 1993, Atlas Film Productions offered investors an opportunity to invest in the movie through a private placement memorandum that outlined terms for a sale of up to 500 limited partnership units at a cost of $100,000 per unit.

The memorandum package included a tape with a short video previewing the message that would be conveyed by the ultimate *Atlas Shrugged* movie. It also listed the individuals who created the offering video and who had been retained as consultants to Atlas Film Productions to work on the movie.

Video trailer and offering circular package

The Atlas Film Productions group included Gloria Alter as associate producer. Alter was a long-time friend of Peikoff and had been stage manager of the 1973 Broadway production of *The Night of January 16th*, Rand's play with alternate endings. Karen Arthur was the director. Arthur was an individual known to both Ayn Rand and Peikoff and, in his agreement of sale of the film rights to Aglialoro, Peikoff stipulated that Arthur was to be hired as director of the *Atlas Shrugged* movie. She had directed two feature length movies, although her primary experience was in television, where she received a Primetime Emmy Award for Outstanding Directing for a Drama Series for her work on *Cagney and Lacey*.

Craig Anderson, of Craig Anderson Productions, was the producer. Anderson was best known at the time for his critically acclaimed 1992 production of Willa Cather's novel *O Pioneers!* with Jessica Lange. He went on to do other adaptations of classic novels and came highly recommended by Arthur.

The money-raising effort was not successful and did not yield the number of interested investors that Aglialoro had anticipated. The terms of the Atlas Film Productions offering provided that if insufficient funds were raised, the money would be returned. Unfortunately, this was the case, and Aglialoro sent back the checks to those who had subscribed.

In the meantime, at the recommendation of Arthur and Andersen, Aglialoro hired Benedict Fitzgerald to write a screenplay. Fitzgerald is an American screenwriter whose writing credits at that time included a television screenplay of *Moby-Dick* and *Wise Blood*. He later co-wrote the screenplay for *The Passion of the Christ* with Mel Gibson. The Fitzgerald *Atlas Shrugged* screenplay was delivered in February 1996, but in the opinion of Aglialoro and, even more vehemently, Peikoff, the screenplay was not as true to the book nor to its message as they felt it needed to be. Partially because of his disappointment with what he perceived as Arthur's failure to come up with an acceptable screenplay, Peikoff released Aglialoro from the requirement to hire Arthur to direct the movie.

Aglialoro at the Cato/IOS event marking the fortieth anniversary of Atlas Shrugged

David Kelley, founder, The Atlas Society

The next screenplay attempt was by Cynthia Peikoff, Leonard's former wife, a writer who had actually served as a typist and secretary for Ayn Rand. Cynthia was intimately familiar with *Atlas Shrugged* and what it stands for. When her script was submitted in early 1997, it was in two acts. Act 1 of the Peikoff screenplay ended with Dagny's plane crash in Galt's Gulch and act 2 completed the story. It called for a movie substantially over three hours in length despite the fact that she had carefully omitted numerous characters and events from the book. And, while the screenplay was faithful to the book, it lacked the drama needed to deliver *Atlas Shrugged* on the big screen and attract the interest of a motion picture studio.

AGLIALORO GETS THE HOOK

1997 was an eventful year in the making of *Atlas Shrugged* into a movie. It was the year in which Aglialoro was asked to resign from the board of the Ayn Rand Institute.

Since initially purchasing the rights in 1992, Aglialoro had often spoken to individuals and groups interested in Ayn Rand and the message of *Atlas Shrugged*. In a typical entrepreneurial fashion, he believed the financial backing for the *Atlas Shrugged* movie was somewhere in the haystack—he just had to find the needle. When Ed Crane, then-president of the Cato Institute, a libertarian think-tank based in Washington, DC, invited him to speak at an event co-sponsored by Kelley's Institute for Objectivist Studies (IOS) and Cato on October 4, 1997, Aglialoro accepted.

It was a celebration of the 40th anniversary of *Atlas Shrugged*. Aglialoro was on the dais with Ed Snider, John Stossel, and Victor Niederhoffer. He looked at it "as an opportunity to gain interest in the movie from an audience that places great value on individual liberty and limited government." Most attendees were admirers of Ayn Rand and had read *Atlas Shrugged*.

Peikoff saw things differently. He quoted Ayn Rand and declared libertarians were radicals and anarchists. Aglialoro argued that today's libertarians are a positive force and bear little resemblance to the libertarians of the 1950s that Rand had condemned. Further, that if Ayn Rand were alive today, she would be in concert with the messages put forth by the majority of libertarian organizations such as Cato.

Despite knowing that this would likely be a break between himself and Peikoff, Aglialoro decided to participate in the Cato event. Peikoff reacted as Aglialoro had expected and, in a phone conversation indelibly imprinted in Aglialoro's memory, Peikoff announced that this was probably the last time they would speak (and it was). He asked that Aglialoro resign from the advisory board of the Ayn Rand Institute, to which Aglialoro reluctantly complied in a letter to Mike Berliner dated September 11, 1997. On a personal basis, Aglialoro said that he felt "an emotional loss" of a real friendship with someone he had admired. Although he had complained frequently about the institute's lack of tolerance, first manifested in the excommunication of Kelley, for anyone who did not adhere to the ARI version of Objectivism, Aglialoro was surprised to find himself among those who were culled from its ranks. Aglialoro now joined a lengthy list of individuals who were once an integral part of the Ayn Rand Institute organization and who, by choice or fiat, were no longer welcome.

Shortly after his departure from ARI in 1997, Aglialoro received a call from Ed Snider, who had resigned from the institute several years prior and was a board member of Kelley's Institute for Objectivist Studies.

Two years later, with Snider's encouragement, Aglialoro accepted the invitation to join the board of IOS (which would soon be named The Atlas Society), where he remains active.

THE TNT AND AL RUDDY YEARS

Originally, Aglialoro thought that the large Hollywood motion picture studios would be interested in producing a movie from a top-selling book such as *Atlas Shrugged*. He soon found out that without a studio-quality script in hand, movie studios had little interest in seriously discussing the opportunity.

However, he thought that producing the book as a miniseries for television might be different. To "shop" the project, in early 1997 he signed an agreement with Gloria Alter, who had previously worked with him on the Atlas Film Productions effort to find financing via the private placement memorandum. Aglialoro knew that Ted Turner, founder of Turner Entertainment, was familiar with *Atlas Shrugged* and thought that Turner Network Television (TNT), a subsidiary of the larger motion picture studio Time Warner, might have an interest.

Alter contacted Al Ruddy (a movie producer Ayn Rand knew and respected), and they approached TNT. Ruddy began working with screenwriter Susan Black and submitted her initial synopsis in February of 1997. Peikoff had reservations about several points he read in the synopsis, but Alter and Ruddy explained that the synopsis is prior to a treatment which is prior to a draft which is prior to a screenplay. Things moved forward and Black continued to refine the screenplay.

After months of negotiations a TNT press release was issued on October 27, 1999, stating: "Ayn Rand's *Atlas Shrugged*, one of the last unproduced epics of the 20th century, will be the subject of a Turner Network Television (TNT) Original movie. Academy Award winner Albert S. Ruddy (The Godfather Trilogy) will executive-produce the four-hour miniseries for Ruddy Morgan Productions. John Aglialoro will also executive-produce, with Gloria Alter producing. The script will be written by Sue Black." The announcement got picked up by a number of trade journals including *Hollywood Reporter* and *Daily Variety*. There were also several stories that appeared in *USA Today*'s Jeannie Williams "This Just In" column, including an offer for readers to express their views on casting—which she forwarded to Ruddy. The response was so overwhelming, the author said, "Much as I have enjoyed hearing from you [Atlas Shrugged fans] don't send me any more email. Please." The article quoted Al Ruddy as stating that Jude Law was a contender for the role of John Galt.

Thus began the next chapter in getting *Atlas Shrugged* to the now-smaller television screen as a miniseries. The Turner organization, as expressed in a February, 2000, letter from Bob DiBetteto, Turner executive vice president, believed that the project was "a daunting task" but one that would produce a memorable movie. To ensure that the film would be true to the essential story and themes of Rand's novel, Aglialoro engaged Kelley as a consultant to review scripts, a role he continues to play.

As Turner Entertainment announced in the press release, Susan Black was selected to write the screenplay. Black had written several successful made-for-TV movies and was well known to Turner. But shortly after the announcement, talk began about a strike—not an *Atlas Shrugged* strike, but a strike of screenwriters. Fearing the Writers Guild of America (WGA) strike would last upwards of six months, Hollywood screenwriters struggled to complete projects that were already in process, and were not even contemplating beginning new ones.

Fear of a strike caused major delays in getting the *Atlas Shrugged* script underway, but a bigger problem came when AOL purchased Time Warner in January of 2001. Time Warner movie executives and their creative teams were consumed with internal issues stemming from the need to merge two very disparate cultures. After agonizing discussions and even more delays, the *Atlas Shrugged* project was abandoned by TNT in March of 2002.

With the TV miniseries no longer an option, Ruddy continued to believe that he could interest a Hollywood studio in the project, and Aglialoro hoped he was right. But, by the end of 2002, with nothing in hand, Aglialoro began to consider other options.

THE BALDWIN ENTERTAINMENT GROUP AND LIONSGATE

When the TNT deal fell apart, Aglialoro began discussions with Crusader Entertainment, LLC, a Beverly Hills-based production company (owned by successful oil entrepreneur Phillip Anschutz). In May 2003, Aglialoro signed an agreement which granted Crusader the right to produce *Atlas Shrugged*. Crusader signed veteran screenwriter James V. Hart, whose movie credits include the adaptation of Carl Sagan's science fiction book *Contact*, to write the screenplay.

Howard Baldwin, president and CEO of Crusader, said in an interview, "I think the box office potential is huge, because of the enormous interest. *Atlas Shrugged* is one of the best-selling books of all time." Less than a year later, Crusader was shut down and the *Atlas Shrugged* project along with it. To keep some of their projects going, the Baldwins (Howard and Karen, a talented husband-and-wife team) set up Baldwin Entertainment Group (BEG), and they continued the effort to develop the *Atlas Shrugged* screenplay with Hart.

As one of the producers of *Ray*, the very well-received biographical movie about the life of Ray Charles, Baldwin was hopeful that *Ray*'s box office success might be helpful in getting a studio to take on *Atlas Shrugged*. For three years, BEG worked diligently to find a studio that would finance and produce the movie.

Finally, in March 2006, BEG succeeded, or so they thought, when Lionsgate Films signed an agreement to produce *Atlas Shrugged*. Not only was Lionsgate a successful studio, responsible for such award-winning pictures as *Girl with a Pearl Earring*, *Crash*, and *Monster's Ball*, but its vice chairman, Michael Burns, was a lifelong *Atlas Shrugged* fan. Burns says he first read the novel in high school and, through the years, has given out over 100 copies as gifts. The novel made such an impact in his life that, when he read Rand's obituary in March 1982, Burns travelled to Valhalla, NY, to attend her funeral.

In an interesting note, Rand had requested that a poem be read at her funeral. The poem was "If" by Rudyard Kipling, and it was read by David Kelley. Kelley had been called upon by Peikoff and Rand herself to read another Kipling poem, "When Earth's Last Picture is Painted," at the funeral of Rand's husband, Frank O'Connor, in 1979.

Lionsgate hired Randall Wallace (*Braveheart, Pearl Harbor, Secretariat*) to write the screenplay. He was interviewed in a January 14, 2007, article that chronicled the journey from the epic novel to the big screen that began in the early 1970s. Wallace echoed the sentiment that originally led Aglialoro to purchase the film rights ("More people will see the movie than will ever read the book"), and the first draft screenplay was delivered in February of 2007.

Vadim Perelman and Howard Baldwin, Atlas Society event, 2007

There was a great deal of public fanfare following a September 21, 2006, article in Daily *Variety* that reported Angelina Jolie was going to appear in the starring role of Dagny Taggart in *Atlas Shrugged*. There were a number of on-going conversations with Jolie's manager, Geyer Kosinksi, and Aglialoro spoke with him on several occasions.

Jolie said that the Dagny character was the most relatable role she had ever read and was particularly interested in the role if the film was going to be directed by Vadim Perelman.

Vadim Perelman (*House of Sand and Fog*) had grown up in the Ukraine under Communist rule. Like Ayn Rand, he was passionate about capitalism, having seen first-hand what life was like without economic freedom. Lionsgate hired Perelman to direct and, basing his script on the Wallace screenplay, Perelman completed the first draft of his script in October of 2007.

Both Perelman and Burns appeared with Aglialoro at a fiftieth anniversary celebration of *Atlas Shrugged* sponsored by The Atlas Society. An October 5, 2007, Washington Times article titled "'Atlas,' at

Last, on Map" quoted Edward Hudgins, then executive director of The Atlas Society: "This is as close as the book has ever come to being filmed."

The fact that Lionsgate was moving forward with hiring Perelman as director and was supporting events such as the Atlas Society anniversary celebration were signs that gave Aglialoro a renewed sense of optimism. This time, he felt certain that *Atlas Shrugged* would begin production—and none too soon because Aglialoro's fifteen-year right to produce the movie was set to expire the following year.

But the optimism proved unfounded. One delay after another kept Lionsgate from getting *Atlas Shrugged* into physical production. The issues were constant and seemed never-ending until, finally, Lionsgate advised Aglialoro that it would not be renewing its option to produce *Atlas Shrugged*.

Burns, nonetheless, maintained an interest in the project and referred Aglialoro to Lionsgate Television to determine whether or not a TV miniseries could be developed. Anticipating a positive outcome as a television series, Aglialoro purchased a two-year extension of the *Atlas Shrugged* movie rights from Peikoff (and later another one-year extension).

In June 2009, Aglialoro signed an agreement with Lionsgate Television that would create *Atlas Shrugged* as a miniseries under the auspices of Epix, a premium TV channel in which Lionsgate was a partner. Writers were hired and they set about writing a treatment. In January 2010, the treatment was delivered. However, upon reading it, Aglialoro was not pleased: the writers planned to combine the life of Ayn Rand, the novelist who grew up in Soviet Russia, with the story of *Atlas Shrugged*. Although the screenplay was interesting, it was not a vehicle to bring the message of the epic novel to the screen, and Aglialoro passed.

So it was over. The rights were set to expire on June 15, 2010, Peikoff would not sell another extension, and Aglialoro had found neither a studio nor anyone else who wanted to finance and produce *Atlas Shrugged*.

But Aglialoro was not going to simply walk away. Particularly not after his wife, Joan Carter, told him that if he did not try to make it happen, "it will haunt you the rest of your life" (a phrase he often quotes when talking about how much pressure he was under to make the movie). There was no other option—he would have to do it himself. After all these years, he would still need to create a screenplay, to find a director, to cast the movie, to secure locations, and, most importantly, to start principal photography; and to get all this accomplished in less than ninety days.

THE MAKING OF ATLAS SHRUGGED

On April 23, 2010, Aglialoro boarded a plane in Philadelphia bound for Hollywood. Earlier in the month, Howard Baldwin had referred him to Harmon Kaslow, an attorney and motion picture industry professional who knew how to get things done. Aglialoro arranged to meet Kaslow the next day and says, "Harmon fell out of the sky."

They agreed that Kaslow would come on board that day to produce the movie along with Aglialoro on the condition that principal photography would start no later than June 15, 2010. Aglialoro had already decided that making *Atlas Shrugged* into a movie was so important that he would commit his own money, and more importantly, his own time to secure the rights and make the movie. The next day they hired a screenwriter and in a week the production staff was twenty. Within a month, the crew had expanded to over one hundred.

However, the issue of making an 1100-page book into a screenplay still needed to be addressed. Knowing from past experience that even the most talented screenplay writers had been unable to do the book justice by condensing it into a single movie script, Aglialoro decided he would follow the three-part structure of the book and produce *Atlas Shrugged* as a trilogy. This meant Aglialoro's entertainment lawyer at Loeb and Loeb, Roger Arar, had to negotiate a new arrangement with Peikoff to pay him royalties on not one, but three, movies.

With the clock ticking, a screenwriter was commissioned to write a screenplay that encompassed only the first part of the book.

They had some good luck and some bad luck:

Good luck was that Hollywood was not booming in the spring of 2010, so talent was available and able to join the production immediately—but not without a great deal of angst. Grant Bowler, who was cast as Henry Rearden, would finish shooting in Australia one day and begin shooting in LA the next. With a twenty-three-hour flight, it was impossible—until the producers realized that Bowler would cross the international date line. This meant he would depart from Australia, fly for twenty-three hours, arrive in Los Angeles the same day, walk off the plane and begin shooting. Any flight delay or other unforeseen event meant that the scene could not take place. In a stroke of good luck, he made it—and Bowler may be the only actor in history who was in two movies on two different continents on the same day.

Another stroke of good luck was Taylor Schilling. Cast as Dagny Taggart, Taylor was working in New York. She boarded a plane for Hollywood on two days' notice to begin filming *Atlas Shrugged*.

Grant Bowler as Hank Rearden and Taylor Schilling as Dagny Taggart

Cast and crew of Atlas Shrugged

In an interesting note, Schilling wore ten different numbered bracelets in the film (replicas are sold online). After the shoot, Aglialoro's wife, Joan Carter, was given No. 1 and the remaining originals he donated to auctions raising money for causes he believes in.

Bad luck was that the first draft screenplay was, as Kaslow put it, "simply unusable."

Good luck was that Brian Patrick O'Toole, a screenwriter, experienced script doctor, and someone familiar with *Atlas Shrugged*, agreed to collaborate with Aglialoro to write the screenplay that ultimately became *Atlas Shrugged*. (Because it has no subtitle, the first movie in the trilogy has become known to insiders simply as *Atlas Shrugged*.)

Bad luck was that, with less than two weeks before expiration of Aglialoro's rights, the first director had to be fired.

Good luck was that Paul Johansson, a friend of Kaslow's and a fan of Ayn Rand, was available and interested in directing with very little time to prepare. His directorial debut in *The Incredible Mrs. Richie* won an Emmy Award.

Johansson's energy and passion was exactly what the producers needed to assemble a cast and crew in such a short amount of time and still be able to produce a theatrical-quality motion picture. Concerned that an event of force majeure (e.g. an earthquake) could delay principal photography and impact Aglialoro's ownership of the rights, a start date of June 13, 2010, was set. Through the hard work of the crew and cast, history was made on that date as Aglialoro's vision of producing *Atlas Shrugged* as a motion picture was realized.

To commemorate the occasion, on June 14, 2010, a full-page ad in *Daily Variety*, the entertainment industry's trade periodical, announced that *Atlas Shrugged*, part 1 of the trilogy, was in principal photography. They had made it.

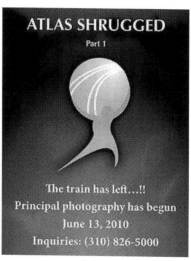

Principal photography!

In order to start production prior to June 15, 2010, Kaslow and Aglialoro quickly became accustomed to doing things simultaneously that were meant to be done sequentially. For example, even after principal photography commenced, not all of the locations had been secured. In fact, the location originally designated for shooting the Rearden Steel factory scenes became unavailable, and the location that ultimately appeared in the movie was secured a mere 24 hours prior to the time shooting occurred. What ended up in the movie is a testament to the talent and hard work of hundreds of crewmembers: they took this location and completely transformed it into Hank's office (and with the magic of a green screen, Rearden's foundry was created in the background).

Aglialoro was particularly concerned that the music be commensurate with the epic nature of the novel. They contacted Elia Cmiral (*Nash Bridges, Ronin, Last Express*) and Aglialoro explained to Cmiral what he was looking for—inspirational with the same feel of majesty as the theme for *Out of Africa*. With the film still in editing, the assignment to create the music was not going to be an easy one. Aglialoro recalled that he went with some trepidation to listen to the score for the first time and it brought tears to his eyes. "Elia just 'got it'," he said. The recording required the right acoustics, which they found in a church in Seattle. Aglialoro says, "To this day, I never tire of hearing the Atlas Shrugged music, particularly the John Galt theme."

Since no studio had the courage to produce Atlas Shrugged, Aglialoro did not count on a studio to have serious interest in distributing the movie, either. To get the film in theaters, Aglialoro challenged Kaslow to create and execute a plan to self-distribute and theatrically release Atlas Shrugged across America. This resulted in the creation of the Atlas Distribution Company, and Aglialoro set April 15, 2011, as an appropriate date to release the movie.

This gave Atlas Distribution almost no time to market and promote the movie, so they turned to technology: the Internet. Actually, the first place they turned was to the growing legion of Atlas Shrugged fans to find someone with Internet and search-engine optimization experience. Their search yielded results when Scott DeSapio, an ardent Objectivist and someone whose life was inspired by Atlas Shrugged, joined the Atlas Shrugged team.

DeSapio quickly began designing a website not only to attract the attention of anyone interested in the movie, but also to insure that Atlas Productions and Atlas Distribution were easy to find through search engine optimization. Before DeSapio took the reins of the company's online presence, the Atlas Shrugged movie Web site was buried on page three in Google. (Note: currently, if you Google "Atlas Shrugged," the number one result is the Atlas Shrugged Movie website.) As more people learned about the movie, Atlas Distribution was flooded with requests from fans to have Atlas Shrugged shown in their hometown theater (as well as in Europe, South America, Asia and Africa). To track this somewhat overwhelming response, DeSapio and his team created a "Demand Atlas" feature on the site which allowed fans to "demand" Atlas Shrugged at a movie theater near them.

There was a lot of excitement among *Atlas Shrugged* fans when it was learned that the movie was actually going to appear in theaters. With neither the time nor money to do the standard P&A (print and advertising), Aglialoro and Kaslow responded to interview requests, using every opportunity to get the story out that *Atlas Shrugged* was going to appear in theaters on April 15, 2011. In addition to the myriad radio interviews, the press was interested in the fact that a most controversial novel was finally going to appear on the big screen. The *Courier Post* (Aglialoro's hometown newspaper) did a full-page spread calling *Atlas Shrugged* "the movie that almost wasn't." The *Philadelphia Inquirer* said the project was "a triumph of will." The *Boston Globe* story named Aglialoro "Ayn Rand's Biggest Fan," and the *Financial Times* published a not-unkind review of the film. *Barron's* wrote a full-page story calling *Atlas Shrugged* the rarest of rare commodities: "a film in which capitalists are the good guys," a statement the producers found gratifying.

As awareness of *Atlas Shrugged* grew, so did interest from theater owners. Atlas Distribution hired Randy Slaughter and Ron Rodgers of Rocky Mountain Pictures to act as its booking agent and to sign up 100 theaters for a "platform" release. However, about thirty days prior to opening, Rocky Mountain was inundated with hundreds of requests from theaters responding to the "demands" of *Atlas Shrugged* fans in their area. Although there was little time to market the film in these new theaters and no time for trailers to be played, Aglialoro approved opening in 400 theaters. When the movie opened with the 3rd highest per-theater gross, Atlas Distribution expanded to 500 theaters. The film ultimately played in 700 theaters, generating nearly $4.7M of box office, which the industry considered outstanding for an independently released movie supported primarily by online marketing.

DeSapio's online efforts paid off in generating awareness. On April 15, 2011, opening day, Google reported that "*Atlas Shrugged*" (for about 3 hours mid-day) was the number-one searched term and Twitter reported *Atlas Shrugged* was its number-three trending topic. DeSapio is now VP of communications for Atlas Productions and is working to continue building awareness of the *Atlas* trilogy. He is also serving as associate producer of *Part III: Who is John Galt?*

Aglialoro was pleased that two very important people in the life of Ayn Rand attended the movie's initial screening in Sony Studios: Nathaniel and Barbara Branden. Both praised the movie and the review by Barbara Branden in *Library of Economics and Liberty*, Aglialoro says, was one of his most uplifting moments in the making of *Atlas Shrugged*. (Barbara, prior to her death in 2014, would also be a script adviser to *Who is John Galt?*)

The premiere was held in Washington, DC's Union Station and Aglialoro was gratified that Ed Snider, his friend and the founder of the Ayn Rand Institute, was in attendance. When the final credits rolled, Snider jumped up and said, "You nailed it!" with a big thumbs-up. The critics, as anticipated, were not so complimentary.

Even though the box office resulted in a successful opening weekend, it never generated the word of mouth every movie hopes for, and *Atlas Shrugged* ultimately lost momentum in the weeks that followed. Nonetheless, the movie was recognized with a number of awards including awards from the Santa Catalina Film Festival (winner –Ronald Reagan Great Communicator Award), the Academy of Science Fiction, Fantasy, and Horror Films (winner–Best DVD Release), and Graphic Design Junction (winner–Best 2011 Movie Poster–For Design Inspiration).

ATLAS SHRUGGED: THE STRIKE

Obviously disappointed by the theatrical revenues, Aglialoro believed he would recoup more of his investment through DVD sales and video on demand. However, he still thought long and hard about whether or not to continue the project by committing to the funding needed to make the second part of the trilogy.

Fortunately, there were others who believed in the importance of bringing the message of *Atlas Shrugged* to the world. Foremost among the group was William A. Dunn—a successful commodities trader/fund manager, who was the chairman of the Reason Foundation at the time. Dunn, along with Aglialoro and six others, made substantial financial commitments in the hope that the second film in the trilogy, *Atlas Shrugged: The Strike*, could be in theaters before the national election November 6, 2012.

The investors, along with Aglialoro himself, viewed *Atlas Shrugged* as a warning about what happens when government takes power and limits economic liberty—and they believed it was a warning that needed to be heard before the American citizens went to the ballot box. With additional funding in hand, Kaslow and Aglialoro set about producing *The Strike* under even more stringent time constraints than they dealt with on *Atlas Shrugged*.

The initial screenplay for *The Strike* was written by a writing team of O'Toole (who was so instrumental in penning *Atlas Shrugged*) and Duncan Scott. Scott is well-known in the Objectivist world for having worked with Rand to edit and promote a movie of the Rand novel *We the Living*. He remained on the set of *The Strike* for most of the shoot and, along with Kelley, served as consultant to ensure that messaging was consistent with Ayn Rand's novel.

The screenplay used as the basis of the shooting script was written by Duke Sandefur (as usual, the final screenplay included producer changes partially to ensure that the message was consistent with the novel). Sandefur had worked with Jeff Freilich, the producer hired by Aglialoro and Kaslow to manage the process of making the film.

Freilich is a Hollywood veteran with a long list of producing credits. He was familiar with *Atlas Shrugged* and had the reputation of delivering films on-time and on-budget. He was the kind of experienced moviemaker the producers needed to meet the very aggressive theatrical release timetable within the financial and time constraints required.

Freilich brought on John Putch to direct. The son of actress Jean Stapleton, Putch began his acting career at age five. He had directed a number of both television and feature films (*Poseidon Adventure*, *Murder 101*, and *Phone Booth*) and won independent film awards. Most

Richard T. Jones (Eddie), Esai Morales (Francisco), Samantha Mathis (Dagny), Jason Beghe (Hank), and Diedrich Bader (Quentin) on a poster for The Strike

importantly for the production of *The Strike*, he had the experience and relationships required to meet a pre-election-day theatrical release.

Casting was a major challenge. In most trilogy movies (*Star Wars* and *Lord of the Rings*, for example), the entire sequence is shot as a single production and the parts are released to theaters separately. This enables the cast to remain constant. In the case of *Atlas Shrugged*, the timeline to secure the rights did not allow negotiation with the actors for anything more than the initial movie. And, after the fact, the producers knew that trying to assemble the same cast was an impossible task. Bowler and Schilling, along with the rest of the cast and crew, had moved on to other projects and the time frame had no provision for adjusting the shooting schedule to accommodate actor availability.

Auditions for the new cast began almost immediately, and the producers were quite happy to land Samantha Mathis in the role of Dagny and Jason Beghe as Rearden. Both are accomplished actors with long lists of credits.

Meantime, the production team was finalizing the screenplay, scouting and constructing sets, and hiring the crews. Despite the additional expense and California's well-documented anti-business environment, Aglialoro decided to again produce *Atlas Shrugged* in Hollywood, which traditionally offers a larger pool of experienced and talented actors and crew.

Like the cast of *Atlas Shrugged*, the first installment of the trilogy, the majority of the cast and crew of *The Strike* had not read the novel. Although not a requirement, the producers felt both the experience and the final result would be enhanced if there was some understanding of the Ayn Rand philosophy. A weekly newsletter was circulated that gave brief overviews of the work as well as a synopsis by David Kelley and others at The Atlas Society.

Concurrent with the production challenges, Aglialoro and Kaslow were faced with the decision of how to theatrically release the film. Should Atlas Distribution hire its own team or outsource it? The decision became easier when they met with Bill Lewis and Russell Schwartz. Lewis—formerly with Summit Entertainment and responsible

Sean Hannity in The Strike

Aglialoro and Kaslow enjoy the moment

for booking the hugely successful *Twilight* motion picture—was available to book *The Strike* in theaters; and Schwartz—formerly of New Line Entertainment and responsible for the *Lord of the Rings* theatrical marketing—was available to lead the theatrical marketing effort.

Armed with a bigger marketing budget than was available for *Atlas Shrugged*, Lewis promptly went about securing more than 1100 theaters for *The Strike*. Schwartz booked more than 1500 television advertisements as well as teaser trailers that played on the Hannity, Rush Limbaugh and Glenn Beck radio shows. Hannity had a cameo role in the film, defending the virtues of Rearden Metal on his "show." DeSapio oversaw the online marketing to the *Atlas Shrugged* community which then numbered more than 150,000 subscribers.

The premiere for *The Strike* was again held in Washington, DC (this time in the Ronald Reagan Building), with a screening in LA a day later. The deadline to release the film a month prior to the US general election was met—and Aglialoro and Kaslow celebrated.

Critics were not invited to see the movie prior to the premiere so there was very little press on opening day. Reviews ranged from a *Reason* magazine article which described the film as "professionally polished" to a *Philadelphia Inquirer* review that gave the movie one star and characterized Galt as displaying "toddler behavior" by deciding "he would rather destroy his toys than share them." (Aglialoro remarked that the message must have hit a sore spot with the liberal author to give three columns of coverage to a one-star movie.)

The box office was disappointing. The tight production schedule had allowed little time to run trailers in the theaters, which is one of the most effective means of generating awareness of and interest in a movie. Thus, most of *Atlas Shrugged: The Strike* marketing focused on TV advertising, radio ads and appearances, and online media.

Despite underperforming in theaters, it did receive recognition from the Moving Picture Institute (awarded—Best Adaptation of an Impossible to Adapt Film) and the Accolade Competition (Award of Merit).

So, what was next?

WHO IS JOHN GALT?: *COMPLETING THE TRILOGY*

Yet again, Aglialoro faced a dilemma: was making the final part of the *Atlas Shrugged* trilogy throwing good money after bad? Why would moviegoers come to see the third part of a trilogy that they didn't care enough about to watch the first two parts of? Was this a triumph of hope over experience?

Aglialoro and his investors—savvy businessmen all—know that money is not made on hope. They also know that if the warning of *Atlas Shrugged* is not heeded in our country, the world Ayn Rand describes in her novel is the inevitable outcome. In which case, the very basis of our economic prosperity—capitalism—is what we stand to lose. With that in mind, the *Part II* investors all agreed to commit their share of *The Strike* proceeds to the third and final movie and, in addition to rolling over his share, Aglialoro agreed to make up the difference.

And so, on February 2, 2013, Aglialoro and Kaslow, without the time constraints faced in producing *Atlas Shrugged* and *The Strike*, began the process once again. The search began for a script for *Atlas Shrugged: Who is John Galt?* to complete the movie trilogy that brings the epic novel of *Atlas Shrugged* to the screen.

Part 3 of Rand's novel is by far the longest in the book. In one paperback edition, part 1, "Non-Contradiction," is 320 pages; part 2, "Either-Or," is 330 pages; but part 3, "A is A," is 435 pages. Part 3 is also the most complex: it is the first appearance of the story's hero, John Galt; it is the love story between Galt and Dagny; and its centerpiece is a 57-page speech given on the radio. The speech is critical to the Objectivist philosophy and to understanding the whole meaning of *Atlas Shrugged*. However, it is not cinematic, nor is it entertaining. The script was going to be challenging to say the least.

There were issues to be addressed.

Would the third part be a stand-alone or would it presume that the viewer had seen the first two movies? Making it a stand-alone would add length since past conversations and events would have to be referenced. As an example, those who saw the prior movies would know who Ellis Wyatt is (a major character in *Part I* but a smaller role in *Part III*). If not, an explanation is needed of who this character is, why he is in Galt's Gulch, and why Dagny obviously respects him. This takes film time that leaves less for the story. Aglialoro and Kaslow ultimately decided on a middle ground. Where possible, characters would have references to put them in context, but the movie would focus on what goes on in part 3.

Would it attempt to enlarge the audience for the Rand message or would it focus on "the base" (ardent fans who know the book and philosophy from cover to cover)?

From the initial purchase of the rights to *Atlas Shrugged* way back in 1992, Aglialoro believed that Rand's message was important to get out to a wider audience. It was why he got involved in the first place. He wanted to introduce the idea that success should be applauded, not resented. That allowing government to continue to strengthen its power will lead to an economic decline from which we will never recover. That we should not feel guilty for being too smart or too good or too rich. These are themes that most people don't think about very often and themes that certainly don't align with what they hear on the nightly news or see in most movies that come out of Hollywood.

So how do you get people into the theater to hear the message of *Atlas Shrugged*? The very people who need to hear it are not likely to come if the movie is a philosophical lecture. However, the love story between Galt and Dagny—that was a theme that could attract a wider audience and was the theme Aglialoro decided to emphasize. Symbolizing the love story, the teaser poster used an image of a sculpture by Michael Wilkerson—an artist whose work was introduced to Aglialoro by Peikoff back in the early days of the Ayn Rand Institute. Wilkerson is an ardent admirer of Rand's writing and, as a sculptor, he is best known for his acrylic works that depict man as a heroic being. Two additional posters were designed to help promote the movie.

There were other issues to be addressed before embarking on the screenplay. Would the final part of the trilogy be a period piece set

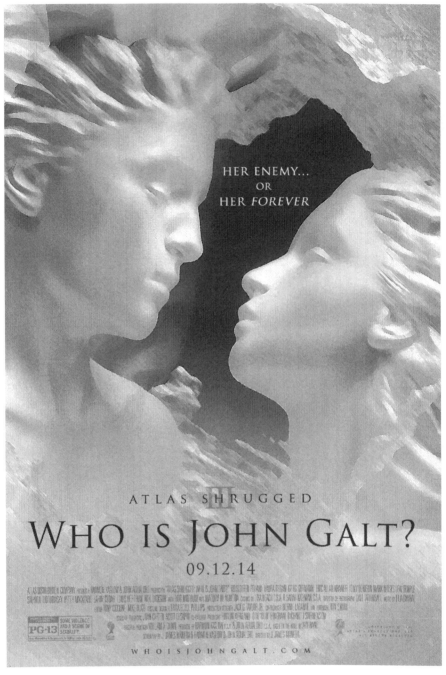

"Heroic Love" poster for Atlas Shrugged: Who is John Galt?

at the time it was written, in 1957? In both prior movies, some fans questioned why there were cell phones and why the wardrobes and autos were obviously of the present day. This was not a difficult decision because Aglialoro had direction from Ayn Rand herself. She had stated to Peikoff, who had told Aglialoro on multiple occasions, that the story of *Atlas Shrugged* is set "the day after tomorrow."

And . . . what do we do about "the speech"? This is the first question Aglialoro is asked when readers of the book hear he is producing the movie. He usually answers that "I plan to have the entire thing read word for word in a dark theater—takes about an hour and a half." And there are Rand fans who think this is a good answer. Obviously not. But Galt's speech is a major challenge. Each and every screenwriter who has dealt with *Atlas Shrugged* throughout the past 25 years has had to find a solution.

The process of developing the screenplay began with initial scripts by Scott (one of the screenwriters for *Part II: The Strike*) and O'Toole (principal writer for *Part I: Atlas Shrugged* and contributor to *The Strike*). Each of the submissions and their multiple revisions had interesting and commendable points, but neither script was what the producers were looking for.

A third writer was hired, Rob Tracinski, former editor of *The Intellectual Activist* (TIA), a publication aligned with the Ayn Rand Institute. Tracinski had stopped working with the institute (citing internal disputes about political issues as one of his reasons) and begun a publication called *The Tracinski Letter*, a newsletter covering politics and culture from an individualist perspective. Actually, Aglialoro and Carter had made a start-up loan through their company, UM Holdings Ltd., to assist Tracinski in launching the newsletter in 2007 and respected his writing skills.

The producers wanted a screenplay that not only was a faithful adaptation of the *Atlas* message, but had a cinematic structure that included the elements of drama and romance depicted in the novel. So, they tasked the newly hired director, Jim Manera, to work with Tracinski and Kaslow to prepare a new screenplay.

Manera is a Hollywood professional who worked on many projects in various roles including *Lombardi*, *The Red Blanket*, and *The Soundtrack of Our Lives*, a 10-part documentary series for PBS/Sony World. He began his career in advertising and has received numerous Clio and other awards for commercials. Manera read *Atlas Shrugged* in college and belongs to The Friends of Abe, Inc., a support and networking group for politically conservative members of the Hollywood elite, formed in 2004 by actor Gary Sinise. "Friends of Abe" is a reference to "Friends of Bill," a group of political friends and donors of former President Bill Clinton, while "Abe" refers to Abraham Lincoln.

Aglialoro, Manera, and Kelley on the set of Atlas Shrugged: Who is John Galt?

Kristoffer Polaha (John Galt)

Working with Kaslow, Aglialoro, DeSapio, and Carter, with almost daily consultation with Kelley, the screenplay took shape. The Galt speech was written and re-written by Kelley and Aglialoro. Even John Stossel made a few edits.

The next step was to hire a casting director and the producers were very pleased when Lisa Beach agreed to cast the movie. She has a long list of credits as casting director including *Wedding Crashers*, *We're the Millers*, and *Horrible Bosses*.

Everyone who reads the book has a vision of *Atlas Shrugged: The Movie* in his or her mind—what the most important themes are, how the characters should look, even who should be cast in what roles. Rand herself thought Faye Dunaway (*Chinatown*, 1974) would be a good Dagny. There are a few of the more orthodox Randians who think that if their vision is not the one that appears on the screen, it is not a good movie. But, by and large, the majority of Ayn Rand fans are realists. They understand that making a movie requires professionals and that finding movie industry professionals who believe in the message of *Atlas Shrugged* is difficult at best. As Aglialoro puts it, "If I have a problem with my toilet, I am looking for a good plumber. I can't worry if he is an Objectivist, although that would certainly be preferable. I need to know he can fix a leak."

In casting John Galt, the producers got really lucky. The moment they saw him and heard him read, the casting director, the director, and the producers agreed: "This is John Galt." Thanks to Lisa Beach, they found a talented actor who had been deeply influenced by Ayn Rand after having read *The Fountainhead* when he was 22. An Objectivist who can fix the leak! He is also incredibly handsome (this author's opinion, but judge for yourself). His name is Kristoffer Polaha, known for *Ringer*, *Life Unexpected*, and *North Shore*.

The next actor to be cast was Dagny. There were a number of talented women who read for the role and the selection was difficult. The decision to cast Laura Regan turned out to be a good one. Regan is a Canadian actress, best known for her role as Jennifer Crane in the

TV series *Mad Men*. She has also had leading and supporting roles in the films *Saving Jessica Lynch*, *My Little Eye*, and *How to Be a Serial Killer*. She had delivered her second baby less than 6 weeks before filming started and already had her figure back.

Laura Regan (Dagny Taggart)

Dinner scene at the Wayne-Falkland Hotel. Left to right: Front: Larry Cedar (Dr. Ferris), Claude Knowlton (Clem Weatherby), Howard Morgan, Peter Lauer, Grover Norquist, Phil Valentine. Back: Harmon Kaslow (producer), Tony Denison (Cuffy Meigs), Jim Manera (director), John Aglialoro (Producer), Louis Herthum (Wesley Mouch)

After the remaining characters were cast, the movie went into pre-production: selecting locations, building sets, finding props, and all the myriad other major and minor tasks that go into creating a film.

A few notables appear in cameo roles in the third movie— people who the producers believe will make their own fans aware when it opens in theaters. Folks like Phil Valentine (radio talk show host in Atlanta—a city which did particularly well at the box office for the first two movies), Grover Norquist (Americans for Tax Reform), Glenn Beck (well-known television personality), Sean Hannity (back by popular demand from *Part II*), Matt Kibbe and Terry Kibbe (FreedomWorks)—individuals who are advancing the cause of liberty, a primary theme of *Atlas Shrugged: Who is John Galt?* And there was a last-minute add of Ron Paul, who turns out to be a pretty good actor, even though he is playing himself.

Contributors to the *Atlas Shrugged* Kickstarter (crowd-funding) campaign also found their way into the movie. Major supporters were invited to the set and the very top supporters got to be extras. Aglialoro gave a lot of thought to whether or not to go forward with a crowd-funding effort. You can always use more advertising money, but, as opposed to most movies that raise money through Kickstarter, this movie was already funded. After deliberation, the producers became convinced that it was a worthwhile effort since it would create awareness that could translate into success at the box office. Simultaneously, it would engage fans whose lives were changed by the message of *Atlas Shrugged* and who wanted to be part of history. Through the years, Aglialoro had received checks—from $25 to $100,000—from *Atlas Shrugged* readers who hoped their participation would get the book to the screen—checks he had always returned. Kickstarter allowed contributors from $1.00 to $10,000 to be part of the movie—and over 3500 are now backers of *Atlas Shrugged: Who is John Galt?*

Of course, nothing ever goes as planned and *Part III* was no exception. For the tunnel scene, the location manager had contracted with the Los Angeles County Metropolitan Transit Authority to use one of the Metro system tunnels for the shoot. The day before filming was scheduled to commence, the producers were shocked to find out that the entire crew would be required to spend three hours in safety training—an expensive proposition, definitely not in the budget. Fortunately, *Atlas Shrugged* had a fan in Los Angeles County Supervisor

Filming the Twentieth Century Motors meeting with Polaha as John Galt

Dominic Daniel (Eddie Willers)

Michael Antonovich, who had come to the set and spent time with Aglialoro trying to figure out how the city could be more hospitable to the film industry. It had not gone unnoticed that less than ten years ago, the vast majority of movies were shot in Los Angeles; today, that number is around 10 percent. Antonovich could not change the tax credit policy of the state of California, but he could help ensure that cast and crew could use the Metro tunnel safely without the burdensome regulatory cost. And he did. He has gone on to propose a number of changes that will streamline permitting and reduce the impact of city regulation for filmmakers.

The set of *Atlas Shrugged* had more visitors than the usual movie production. In addition to Kickstarter donors and supporters of *Atlas Shrugged* from libertarian and conservative groups, the producers sponsored internships for ten members of the Students for Liberty (SFL) organization. SFL's president, Alexander McCobin, was an extra in the Twentieth Century Motors scene where Galt announces he will "stop the motor of the world."

Brian Doherty from *Reason* magazine appeared on-set and did a full day of interviews, including a discussion with Dominic Daniel, who plays Eddie Willers. Doherty's article on Reason.com explains that Daniel read *The Fountainhead* in high school and the message resonated with him. He said, "That book spoke about individuality, finding one's own path and taking responsibility for your own life and not listening to people who say 'you owe it to us.'" Daniel knows there are a lot of curious feelings and even some hostility toward Rand's work in Hollywood and admits he has friends who are not fans. But "I didn't have any reservations," says Daniel. Aglialoro and Kaslow are quick to add that they had no reservations either and casting Daniel as Eddie Willers was a perfect match.

Filming ran a few days over schedule. Although the cast and crew worked hard to meet the target, it was a very aggressive plan.

With shooting complete, the process began of assembling the raw footage into a film. Manera delivered the director's cut on April 15th, at which time the producers, associate producers, DeSapio and

Carter, and the entire post-production team began the editing process that would tell the story they envisioned. Elia Cmiral (*Part I*'s composer) was recruited to do the music and the special effects people began their work. The producers were very happy to be able to get Sam Nicholson of Stargate Studios (*Ghostbusters*, *Star Trek II*) to handle special effects.

At the same time, Atlas Distribution got into gear and Bill Lewis (general sales manager for *The Strike*) came back on board to start planning where the movie would open. Using attendance on a per theater basis from *Parts I* and *II*, he started telling selected exhibitors that he would be bringing them *Part III* of the *Atlas Shrugged* trilogy to open in September. He also introduced the teaser trailer "sand art," designed to pique the interest of moviegoers—some of whom have read the book, but most of whom have not.

WAS IT WORTH IT?

Making *Atlas Shrugged* into a movie has been a long and winding road. Aglialoro is often asked if it has been worth it. Was it worth getting turned down by every movie studio in the country? Was it worth spending all those months in Los Angeles and the hundreds of flights back and forth from East to West Coast? Was it worth risking all that money—and maybe losing a good chunk of it when all is said and done? Was it worth the disappointment of knowing that what you care about so deeply is just not worth a $10.00 movie ticket to millions of Americans?

His answer is yes. It was worth it.

Says Aglialoro, "I had an obligation. I was the one who had held out hope that the movie could be made and that the message of Ayn Rand could help save our country. I was the one who wanted to see businessmen as heroes. I was the one who made her a silent promise. There was no one else to do it. I can go to her grave now and know that I did my best."

The version of this "History" published as a separate ebook contains links to many relevant documents.

The man who is John Galt and the man who made it happen
take in part of the world of Atlas Shrugged

Character	Part I	Part II	Part III
Dagny Taggart	Taylor Schilling	Samantha Mathis	Laura Regan
Hank Rearden	Grant Bowler	Jason Beghe	Rob Morrow
Lillian Rearden	Rebecca Wisocky	Kim Rhodes	
Francisco d'Anconia	Jsu Garcia	Esai Morales	Joaquim de Almeida
John Galt	Paul Johansson	D.B. Sweeney	Kristoffer Polaha
James Taggart	Matthew Marsden	Patrick Fabian	Greg Germann
Eddie Willers	Edi Gathegi	Richard T. Jones	Dominic Daniel
Gwen Ives	Nikki Klecha	Jennifer Cortese	
Ellis Wyatt	Graham Beckel		Lew Temple
Wesley Mouch	Michael Lerner	Paul McCrane	Louis Herthum
Hugh Akston	Michael O'Keefe		Stephen Tobolowski
Robert Stadler	Navid Negahban	Robert Picardo	Neil Dickson
Midas Mulligan	Geoff Pierson		Mark Moses
Floyd Ferris		John Rubinstein	Larry Cedar
Mr. Thompson		Ray Wise	Peter MacKenzie
Jeff Allen		Jeff Yagher	Jeff Yagher
Cherryl Taggart		Larisa Oleynik	Jen Nikolaisen
Ragnar Danneskjöld			Eric Allen Kramer
Eugene Lawson	Rob Brownstein		Phil Valentine
The Wet Nurse		Bug Hall	
Clem Weatherby		Stephen Macht	Claude Knowlton
Kip Chalmers		Rex Lynn	
Phillip Rearden	Neill Barry		
Jay Knight	Dave Goryl		
Paul Larkin	Patrick Fischler		
Quentin Daniels		Diedrich Bader	
Ken Danagger		Arye Gross	
Orren Boyle	Jon Polito		
Thomas Hendricks			Scott Klace
Cuffy Meigs			Tony Denis

WHY ARE THERE DIFFERENT CASTS FOR *ATLAS SHRUGGED?*

DAVID KELLEY

The *Atlas Shrugged* trilogy employed more than a hundred actors in speaking roles across all three parts. The accompanying table of principal and secondary roles is a partial list. Many of the actors were familiar, chiefly from work in television. Some have gone on to leading roles, like Taylor Schilling, who played Dagny in *Part I* and now is the lead in *Orange is the New Black*.

The films included appearances by non-Hollywood celebrities such as commentators Sean Hannity, Bob Beckel, Juan Williams, Glenn Beck, Phil Valentine, and Andrew Walkow; Judge Alex Kozinski; Teller (of Penn & Teller); and activist Matt Kibbe.

But the most significant feature of the casting is that characters who appeared in more than one part were played by different actors. Many people have asked why.

Unlike the James Bond franchise, multi-part adaptations from a single literary work or series tend to use the same cast throughout. That's true of *The Lord of the Rings*—a model that the *Atlas* team often discussed—and of *The Godfather*. Why not *Atlas Shrugged*?

The answer requires a bit of history. When John Aglialoro decided to do the film adaptation as an independent production, after a long series of unsuccessful efforts in partnership with studios like Lionsgate, his option was about to expire. In early April 2010, after the last Lionsgate effort collapsed, he took the plunge. He teamed up with veteran producer Harmon Kaslow. Over the next two months they formed a production company; opened an office in Los Angeles; created the script, which Aglialoro co-wrote with Brian Patrick O'Toole; hired the production team and crew; auditioned talent; and lined up locations for shooting the film. Paul Johansson signed on as director just nine days before filming was to begin, after the first director was fired. Cameras rolled on June 13, two days before the deadline.

That is an astonishing achievement. But it had its costs. *The Lord of the Rings*, with a budget of $285 million and eight years in production, could afford to film all three parts at the same time, with the same cast. That was not a luxury Aglialoro and Kaslow had. With a budget under $15 million and a two-month deadline, there was no way to do more than the first part. As Kaslow has explained, "When we set out to make *Part I* we had a ticking clock where if we didn't start production by a certain date John's interest in the rights could lapse. We didn't have the luxury at that moment to negotiate future options with the various cast members." The rest of the story would have to wait.

A CLEAN SWEEP

After the theatrical release, the team moved on to planning *Part II*. But the need for a larger budget, especially for promotion, meant lining up outside investors, which took until early 2012. And the critical response to *Part I*, though chiefly hostile to the ideas, did highlight some shortcomings of the hasty production. In the circumstances, the producers decided on a clean sweep.

In any film, the actors are the visible connection with the audience. But the artistic quality of a film—its visual power and impact for an audience—depend at least as much on those behind the camera: the screenwriter, the director, and the heads of cinematography, production design, art, and music. Indeed, a film is normally cast in terms of who can best work with a previously chosen director to enact a pre-determined script. In *The Lord of the Rings* and *The Godfather*, all of these other roles, along with the cast, were filled by the same people in all three parts.

By the same token, it is not just the cast that has changed in *Atlas*. The clean sweep included additional writers, a new director, and new people in the other key roles in *Part II*; the sweep was nearly as clean in *Part III*.

Reassembling the cast from *Part I* for all the speaking roles would have been a near-impossible task, especially since the producers were committed—in early 2012—to have *Part II* in theaters by October. Without a previously negotiated contract, the actors understandably moved on to other projects. Reassembling the whole cast would have been difficult enough, and potentially costly. Reassembling them along with the other principals would have been an order of magnitude more difficult. And, frankly, there were good reasons to replace some of the behind-the-camera people.

THE LEARNING CURVE

We should remember, too, the learning curve that the producers have traced. In part, that curve was a consequence of Aglialoro's inexperience in moviemaking, along with the severe pressures of time and budget. With *Part I* completed and the rights secured, he and his colleagues had more time to learn from experience and put it to use in planning the next installments.

Anyone filming *Atlas Shrugged* would have to experiment and learn from his first efforts about how best to adapt this unique work. That's one reason why it has taken over half a century to bring *Atlas* to the screen.

Atlas Shrugged is a long novel. And unlike Lord of the Rings—also a long work—it does not consist in a single quest with episodic challenges along the way. It is tightly plotted, with nested events, complex interactions among characters, and mysteries that build from frame to frame. The core of its plot is not the victory of one family's gang over others (Godfather), nor a series of fanciful battles against imaginary monsters (Lord of the Rings), but a mystery story about the role of reason in man's existence and the assault on man's soul by bad ideas.

IMAGINING THE CHARACTERS

Fans of Atlas Shrugged who have seen all three parts will have their favorites for the various roles. But I urge you to consider one overarching thought. Those of us who love the novel have created images of the characters in our minds. The task of the film is not to reproduce those images. There's no way to do that. The producers' task is to create an adaptation in which the actors can bring Rand's epochal theme and narrative to life.

The actors who played Dagny, Hank, Francisco, and other characters brought different interpretations to their respective roles, revealing new dimensions of the characters, enlarging our understanding of them. And the most important element in Rand's novel is the theme. As Kaslow says, "The message of Atlas is greater than any particular actor, so it's one of those pieces of literature that doesn't require in our view an interpretation by a singular actor."

AYN RAND'S WORLD

In the end, the central character of the films is the world Rand created. In notes she made while writing the novel, she made the arresting assertion that the focus was to be about the world, not about the characters as individuals:

> Theme: What happens to the world when
> the prime movers go on strike. . . .

The first question to decide is on whom the emphasis must be placed—on the prime movers, the parasites, or the world. The answer is: the world. . . .

In this sense, [*Atlas Shrugged*] is to be much more a "social novel" than *The Fountainhead*. . . . In *The Fountainhead* I showed that Roark moves the world—that the Keatings feed upon him and hate him for it, while the Tooheys are consciously out to destroy him. But the theme was Roark—not Roark's relation to the world. Now it will be the relation. . . .

In *The Fountainhead* I did not show how desperately the world needed Roark—except by implication. . . . It was Roark's story. This must be the world's story—in relation to the prime movers.

Rand did not carry through consistently on the intention to make the world the centerpiece, rather than her characters. She created heroes of startling individuality and stature, and villains representing distinctive varieties of human evil. But her overarching theme of a world perishing from the growth of power and loss of freedom—and its meaning for her fictional world as well as for our own—is the essential standard for any film adaptation.

In my judgment, the cast changes are compatible with this standard. And if the changes help audiences abstract the message from the characters portrayed by the cast, they will have proved valuable.

SCRIPTING THE SPEECHES IN *ATLAS SHRUGGED*

DAVID KELLEY

A*tlas Shrugged* is a novel of ideas. Those ideas are conveyed primarily through the traits of the characters, their conflicting goals, and the actions they take in pursuit of those goals. But the ideas are also voiced explicitly. The plot has the form of a detective story: the protagonists Dagny Taggart and Hank Rearden struggle to solve the mysteries they confront. Conventional stories of this type often end with the detective's explanation of the crime and the culprit. Since the mystery in *Atlas Shrugged* is ultimately philosophical, the explanation—as well as many of the clues along the way—takes the form of philosophical exposition.

These moments are the famous speeches, culminating in Galt's speech. Even the shortest speeches are much too long to be reproduced in a film adaptation. In the novel, a reader can pause in the middle to reflect on the ideas, jump ahead to the continuation of the action, or come back to reread. The moviegoer has no such luxury. Film is a medium with a shorter duration and a faster pace of continuous action and interaction, and—at least in the theater—no opportunity for the viewer to pause or go back.

Nevertheless, the speeches are events that play an important role in the narrative, important enough to be included in the film. They have effects on the characters, and they move the plot forward. The challenge for the screenwriters in the *Atlas Shrugged* trilogy was to convey the essential content of the speeches in the briefest possible form.

As the consultant tasked with ensuring that the films are true to the essential ideas of the novel, I paid special attention to the speeches and worked with the writers on each of them. We relied on the following criteria in developing the script:

- The speech must have a clear significance for the characters and the action. It must make sense for the speaker to be saying these words at this moment, in this situation.
- The speech must convey the core ideas but exclude all the secondary points and elaborations in the novel.
- The speech must articulate only those ideas that have been dramatized in previous scenes or will be dramatized in later scenes (if those scenes somehow evoke the viewer's memory of the speech).
- The language must be simple, clear, and powerful. It should use iconic lines from the novel but paraphrase other points in contemporary, evocative, concrete words.

How did we do? I have reproduced the scripts for three speeches that correspond directly to speeches in the novel— Francisco's "money speech," Hank Rearden's response to the judges at his trial, and Galt's speech—and I have offered comments on how and why they were adapted as they were. To indicate the scale of reduction, I have given the number of words in the dialogue and the word count of the corresponding passage in the novel.

(In what follows, the dialogue corresponds exactly to the final version of the films, after editing wrapped up. Scripts also include stage directions about settings and actions, but these are hardly more than suggestions to the director, cinematographer, and editor; and they rarely provide much information about what the viewer actually sees. We have included only directions that are useful in understanding the dialogue.)

FRANCISCO'S MONEY SPEECH (PART II)

This speech occurs at the wedding of James Taggart and Cherryl Brooks, adapted from chapter 2 of part 2 of the novel.

> JAMES TAGGART
>
> Money cannot buy happiness. Truer words were never spoken. We're no longer chasing the almighty dollar. Our ideals are higher than profit. Instead of the aristocracy of money, we have --
>
> FRANCISCO (Off-screen)
>
> -- the aristocracy of pull.
>
> FRANCISCO (CONT'D)
>
> I mean, now it's about influence. But you knew that already.

We hear murmuring.

> JAMES TAGGART
>
> What I know is that you need to learn some manners.
>
> RECEPTION GUEST #1
>
> If you ever doubted that money was the root of all evil, there's your proof.

Francisco pushes through. To GUEST #1:

> FRANCISCO
>
> Oh, so you think money is "the root of all evil"? Have you ever

asked yourself, what's the root of money? Money is a tool that allows us to trade with one another. Your goods for mine. Your efforts for mine. The keystone of civilization. Having money is not the measure of a man. What matters is how he got it. If he produced it by creating value, then his money is a token of honor.

                    JAMES

Look who's talking about honor.

        FRANCISCO (ignoring James)

But if he's taken it from those who produce, then there is no honor. Then you're simply a looter.

    RECEPTION GUEST #2 (condescendingly)

Señor d'Anconia, we all know money is made by the strong at the expense of the weak.

Francisco moves to face GUEST #2.

                    FRANCISCO

What kind of strength are you talking about? The power to create value? Or the ability to manipulate, to extort money in backroom deals -- to exercise pull?

                JAMES TAGGART

Just leave!

                    FRANCISCO

When money ceases to be the tool by which men deal with one

```
another,  then  men  become  the
tools  of  men.  Blood,  whips,
chains  --  or  dollars.  Take  your
choice  --  there  is  no  other  --
and your time is running out.
```
Word count: 257. Novel: 2,793

The Taggart wedding is a gathering of the crony "capitalist" elite and their enablers in government—those who have grown rich through political manipulation rather than honest production. It is the perfect setting for Francisco to appear and to name their essence, drawing the distinction between makers and takers. His purpose in speaking is partly to put them on notice that he understands the nature of their game. In the novel, there's a long stretch between his opening salvo ("the aristocracy of pull") and the speech itself, during which Francisco tells James how much he knows about a scheme by James and his cronies to invest in d'Anconia Copper and then drive up the stock by placing restrictions on competitors —an example of how such looters get rich through pull. The film could not go into that subplot, but the accusation is still telling.

Francisco's other and more important purpose has to do with Dagny and Hank, the two genuine producers in the scene. He is letting them know that he is not one of the looters, and he is giving them, especially Hank, the words to understand the moral issues in their battle against people like James. That he has succeeded in that purpose is shown in Rearden's trial speech shortly thereafter.

The script includes the two essential ideas from the novel: that money, as a medium of exchange, reflects the principle that people should trade value for value; and that those values—the goods and services we trade—have to be produced. The only other idea from the novel is a response to the claim that the strong exploit the weak, but Francisco uses his response ("What kind of strength are you talking about?") primarily to repeat and reinforce the distinction between makers and takers. In the novel, he makes a number of other points: the role of the mind in production, the moral right of individuals to work for their own benefit, and the ethics of inheritance, among others. But all those points were excluded from the script because they were made explicit elsewhere, or had no relevance to the narrative, or simply were not important enough to deserve precious screen time.

The film version opens and closes with memorable lines from the novel:

> Have you ever asked, what is the root of money?

And:

> When money ceases to be the tool by which men deal with one another, then men become the tools of men. Blood, whips, and chains—or dollars. Take your choice—there is no other—and your time is running out.

In between, we paraphrased the novel in "man in the street" terms. I would have wished for more exposition of the core ideas, but cinematic reasons required us to keep it brief.

Notice that we invoked the idea of money earned as "a token of honor" from the second paragraph of the novel's version, but used it to create an exchange among characters (James: "Look who's talking about honor.") That too was a cinematic call. In a film, the camera cannot stay on a character's face for minutes on end while he delivers his thoughts, nor show the rest of the cast in static listening mode. So interactive exchanges were built into the script.

REARDEN'S TRIAL SPEECH (PART II)

This speech is adapted from chapter 4 of part 2 of the novel. The "Fair Share" regulation, imposed at the end of part 1, required Hank Rearden to sell Rearden Metal to all customers in equal (very low) quantities. But in a secret deal, Readen has sold more than that amount to coal producer Ken Danagger. Their deal has been discovered by the government; both men are indicted, but Danagger disappears and Hank is left to face trial.

JUDGE BECKSTON

Henry Rearden, you are charged, along with Kenneth Danagger, in absentia, with one count of violation of Article Sixty-Four of the Fair Share Law. Specifically, the illegal sale and transfer of four thousand tons of strategic material known as "Rearden Metal" to Kenneth Danagger and Danagger Coal.

How do you plead, sir?

REARDEN

I do not recognize this court's right to try me, nor do I recognize any of my actions as a crime.

A BEAT -- murmurs from the gallery.

JUDGE BECKSTON

Mr. Rearden, you will have to enter a plea before this court. Simply refusing to obey the law is not a defense.

REARDEN

If you believe you may seize my property simply because you need it . . . Well then, so does any burglar. The only difference is a burglar doesn't ask my permission.

JUDGE BECKSTON

Sir, I will remind you the punishment this court might impose on you is severe.

REARDEN

Go ahead. Impose it.

If you sentence me to jail, send armed men to get me. I will not volunteer to go. If you fine me, you'll have to seize my assets. I will not volunteer to pay. If you feel you have the right to use force against me, then show it for what it is -- bring guns.

JUDGE BECKSTON

Sir, we have no intention of pointing guns and seizing your property.

REARDEN

Then why are we here?

Judge Giesie can't contain herself.

JUDGE GIESIE

Mr. Rearden, you are misrepresenting the letter and the intent of the Fair Share Law. It is based on the highest principle -- the principle of the "public good."

REARDEN

As defined by those who would dictate and regulate our behavior -- in our homes and our businesses -- stealing their power from our liberty.

Much APPLAUSE.

JUDGE BECKSTON

Gallery will come to order.

JUDGE GIESIE

Mr. Rearden, you wouldn't want it misunderstood that you work for nothing but your own profit?

REARDEN

Indeed, I want it understood clearly.

I do not recognize the good of others as a justification for my existence.

If their fair share demands that I get nothing for my labors -- that it requires me to be a victim -- then I say: public good be damned. I'll have no part of it.

JUDGE BECKSTON

And how does that benefit your fellow man?

REARDEN

I do not owe you an answer, but I could tell you in a hundred ways: thousands of jobs, billions in revenue, fueling our economy despite your efforts to destroy the very foundation of our existence.

And I believe most of my fellow men would say the same if they had a voice.

The courtroom erupts in APPLAUSE.

JUDGE BECKSTON

Another outburst and I will clear the court.

Beckston covers the microphone with his hand and turns to speak with the other JUDGES.

> JUDGE BECKSTON (<u>sotto voce</u>)
>
> Putting this sonovabitch in jail is suicide. The S-S-I will never get their metal.

> JUDGE GIESIE (S.V.)
>
> No, we need an example, not a martyr.

> JUDGE BECKSTON (S.V.)
>
> We can't set a precedent here -- not with this man.

> JUDGE BECKSTON (CONT'D)
>
> Mr. Rearden, on your behalf the court has entered a plea of "no contest" and this panel has found you guilty.

A ripple through the courtroom. A little APPLAUSE.

> JUDGE BECKSTON (CONT'D)
>
> You are hereby sentenced to ten years in prison and a fine of fifty million dollars.
>
> Sentencing of Kenneth Danagger will be withheld pending his appearance before this body.

(beat; to Rearden)

> Now, Mr. Rearden, taking into consideration your distinguished achievements, your contributions to society, and your full cooperation in this matter, your sentence is suspended. This court is now adjourned.

The   JUDGES   retreat.   APPLAUSE   erupts   in   the
courtroom.

Word count: 530. Novel: 2,511

    The trial of Hank Rearden plays two important roles in the narrative. The first is to mark a transition in the growth of political control over producers. Up to this point, Hank's enemies have worked against him primarily by indirect means, mostly out of public view. But his refusal to comply (as by his refusal to sell his metal to the State Science Institute) leads them to bring a criminal charge against him in what amounts to a public show trial, a significant step in the looters' pursuit of unbridled power. The trial also marks a transition in Hank's understanding of the "sanction of the victim" principle, the principle that we should not sanction—i.e., support or endorse—the actions of those who treat us unjustly. In the previous chapter (and a few scenes earlier in the film), Francisco had given him the clue: If the world is crushing him, Atlas, the Titan condemned to carry it on his shoulders, should shrug. Here we see that Rearden got the message.

    During his back-and-forth with the judges, Hank employs the principle in two ways. He refuses, first of all, to sanction the proceeding as an exercise of law. In lines drawn directly from the novel, he denies the court's right to try him for what was a morally honest business deal, and he refuses to help the authorities pretend that they are engaged in anything but a naked exercise of force. When he challenges them to "bring guns," they recoil defensively, proving their need for him to cooperate in his own victimization. The final exchange among the judges as they privately discuss what to do with Rearden (an exchange added by the screenwriters—it is not in the novel) nicely emphasizes how arbitrary and politicized the trial is.

    Hank also refuses to sanction the moral premise invoked by the judges: the primacy of "the public good" and the obligation to "benefit your fellow man." In the novel, Hank gives a ringing defense of his right to work and live for himself. He explains that his wealth came from voluntary transactions with others:

> I work for nothing but my own profit—which
> I make by selling a product they need to men
> who are willing and able to buy it. I do not
> produce it for their benefit at the expense of
> mine, and they do not buy it for my benefit
> at the expense of theirs; I do not sacrifice my
> interests to them nor do they sacrifice theirs
> to me; we deal as equals by mutual consent to
> mutual advantage—and I am proud of every
> penny that I have earned in this manner.

On this second issue of sanction, the script is less successful than for the procedural issue of law. Hank's response to the judge who invokes the public interest—

> As defined by those who would dictate and
> regulate our behavior—in our homes and our
> businesses—stealing their power from our
> liberty—

is a bit awkward, and does not really hit the nail on the head. That "the public interest" is determined by the interests of those in power is true but not essential. The essential objection is that it is used to subordinate the individual to the collective.

In the novel, moreover, Hank explains that he has done more good for others than the government has, and that their policies are not serving the public good. But he refuses to offer these points in his defense because he will not make his right to live contingent on service to others. "If it were true that men could achieve their good by means of turning some men into sacrificial animals . . . I would refuse. I would reject it as the most contemptible evil." The script makes these same points, but in reverse order: In response to Judge Giesie's invocation of "the public good," Hank says "I do not recognize the good of others as the justification for my existence." Then, in response to Beckston's question how his pursuit of profit "benefit[s] your fellow man,"

Rearden explains the economic benefits he has showered on others. Although giving him the opening line "I don't owe you an answer" is a nod to the logic of the speech in the novel, ending with the benefits to others rather than his right to his own existence weakens the speech philosophically. But it does make sense cinematically: Hank's reference to "my fellow men" offsets Beckston's words, invoking the benevolent spirit of independent individuals rather than victims needing alms, and sets up the cheering response of Hank's fellow men in the courtroom audience.

GALT'S SPEECH (PART III)

In his radio speech (in part 3, chapter 7 in the novel), John Galt takes over the airwaves from the Head of State Thompson and reveals the strike to the public, demanding a radical change in direction before the strikers will return. For the film, the speech was updated to television.

While he is speaking, Galt cannot be fully visible, so he appears in shadows, just barely recognizable to the film audience (and to Dagny). The camera cuts away from him at times to show people reacting to his words, but he speaks continuously in voice-over during these cutaways. He is not interacting with anyone, as Francisco and Hank were in the previous speeches. We have therefore presented the script as a continuous flow without stage directions.

GALT

Ladies and gentlemen, Mr. Thompson will not speak to you tonight. His time is up.

For years, you have asked: Who is John Galt? You have asked that question in despair and resignation as factories closed, goods became scarce, jobs disappeared. Your lives are

becoming more difficult as the
life-force of your world is
draining away. You have asked
that question without expecting
an answer. I am here to answer
it.

This is John Galt speaking.

Mr. Thompson won't tell you the
truth about the crisis in your
world. I will.

Have you noticed that as
everything around you seems to
decline, one thing still grows?
It is the power of your rulers.

None of their plans and directives have [sic] solved your
problems or made your life better. The only result has been
their increased control over you
at the cost of your freedom. Do
you know why?

You gave them the power. They
called for your sacrifice, and
you thought it was noble.

They said if you worked for
yourself, and your family, that
you were selfish, and uncaring.
And they made you feel ashamed.

They denounced the leaders of
industry as greedy exploiters --
the Ellis Wyatts, the Hank Reardens -- and again you agreed.

And then you ask: Why did they,
and others like them, disappear?
I took them from you.

Their achievements flowed from their creative minds. Once they understood that the attempt to control their work was an attempt to control their minds, they left.

The people on strike worked for themselves, for their own vision of what was possible. When they recognized the honor they deserved, they rebelled against the guilt you wanted them to feel for their success. You counted on them to keep producing, to keep thinking -- even as you denounced them as selfish. I showed them they were being punished for their own virtues -- and I showed them how evil that is. I made it my mission to help these heroes say no. All evil needs to win is the consent of good people.

They have joined me to freely produce, trade, cooperate, and compete, in a place where the rights of all are protected.

Do not try to find us. Do not try to bargain for our return. Get out of our way. To everyone within the range of my voice, you now have a choice to make.

If you decide to support the notion of sacrifice, enforced by the state, your game is up. Your world is in a downward spiral, and you will ride it down to destruction.

But if you share the values of our strike . . . if you believe that your life is a sacred possession, for you to make the most of . . . if you want to live by the judgment of your own mind, not edicts from the state, then follow our lead. Do not support your own oppressors. Stop letting the system exploit you. Form your own communities on the frontiers of your crumbling world.

Your rulers hold you by your endurance to carry the burdens they impose; by your generosity when you hear cries of despair; and above all, by your innocence, which cannot grasp the depths of their evil. The world you are living in is the world they wanted. Leave them to it.

Those who have left you are eager to build a better world, a world of freedom and opportunity, a world based on mutual respect.

In that world, you will rise in the morning with the spirit you knew in childhood: the spirit of eagerness and adventure -- and the confidence that the world is what it is and is there for you to discover. In that world, you will not receive alms, nor pity,

```
nor forgiveness of sins -- but
honor, respect, and justice.

Don't let the fire go out, spark
by irreplaceable spark, in con-
fusion and despair.

Be sure of your path. The world
you  desire  can  be  won,  it
exists, it is real, it is pos-
sible, it is yours.
```

Word count: 670. Novel: 32,882

In the novel, Galt's speech is a long explanation of the philo-sophical reasons for the strike, including Rand's first statement of her systematic philosophy, Objectivism. Galt also mounts a fundamental assault on the premises and culture of mysticism, altruism, and collect-ivism. At 60-plus pages, the speech is far too long even to summarize in the film. Fans of the novel have often asked how a film could possibly handle the speech. As the word counts indicate, the script required a vast reduction in content. In terms of time, a three-hour speech was reduced to four and a half minutes.

We achieved this result by adhering strictly to our general cri-teria. First and foremost, the script had to be governed by the narrative role of the speech. The strategy of Galt's strike is based on his insight that the altruist-statist system is sustained only by the implicit sanction of the producers: their *material* sanction in working within the system and their *moral* sanction in failing to challenge its premises. Galt and his fellow recruiters have led the top producers to withdraw their material sanction by ceasing to produce. They did this secretly, in the expectation that their withdrawal would cause the economy to decline, and the looters' power to grow, to the point where the terrible con-sequences are evident to everyone. At that point, the strategy requires that Galt explain the strike to the world, stating explicitly the with-drawal of *moral* sanction, demanding freedom and respect for produ-cers, and inviting all good people to join the strikers' cause.

So the speech had to achieve three objectives:

1. The what: Galt must introduce himself and reveal the strike.
2. The why: He must explain why the altruist-statist system is both unjust and destructive.
3. The call to action: He must rally people to join the strike and build a better world.

In the novel, most of the speech is concerned with point 2, as Galt presents a new philosophy and explains what is wrong with the world. The writers went over the structure of the speech (see my "Outline of Galt's Speech," this volume) to identify the points that had to be included and could be conveyed succinctly. One criterion was to include only those ideas that had been dramatized in the action and characters. The premises of the mind-body dichotomy, for example, which the novel explores primarily through the character of Hank Rearden, and which Galt discusses at length, are not a significant theme in the film.

The same is true of the conflict between reason and mysticism, another focus of Galt's speech in the novel. To be sure, Galt has earlier described the strikers as "men of the mind." He has demonstrated in action his own commitment to reason and objectivity. And the script included a nod to the theme:

> Their achievements flowed from their creat-
> ive minds. Once they understood that the
> attempt to control their work was an attempt
> to control their minds, they left.

But we did reduce the focus on this theme because outright, explicit mysticism played no part in the film's narrative. The epistemological sins of the villains ran more to short-range pragmatism and evasion. We did not need Galt to explain that those are irrational; that's obvious, especially to an American audience.

What *had* been dramatized—extensively and throughout all parts of the trilogy—was the rejection of altruism and the demand for freedom, along with the "sanction of the victim" principle. So they were the major focus in trying to meet the second objective.

A further consideration was that these points had been stated explicitly in the Galt's Gulch scenes, in Dagny's conversations with Galt, Akston, and others. So of course the audience has heard them, too. Scripting the speech therefore required a delicate balance between the need to explain the strike to the world at large, as the narrative required, and the risk of losing the viewer's engagement by repeating themes unnecessarily. This dramatic need was aided by frequent inter-cuts to the reaction of people in the studio where Head of State Thompson was to broadcast his speech and of people in the streets, in bars, and in their workplaces.

One way we handled the severe condensation of ideas was to invoke well-known tropes. In the passage describing the strike, for example, we have the line, "All evil needs to win is the consent of good people." That way of putting it does not capture the depth of the sanc-tion-of-the-victim principle in the novel's version of the speech. But what it lacks in depth is offset by the instant recognition of the theme.

In the film, points one and three are at least as important as two. To work in the film, the speech has to be a *speech*, not a lecture. Galt's revelation of the strike must be bold and startling enough to arrest the attention of the people watching in the street and to terrify the power-brokers in the studio. And his call to action must be highly motivating—a philosophical sales pitch powerful enough to galvanize the characters in the film as well as the film audience.

In this respect, we had the advantage of Rand's iconic lan-guage. It was clear going in that we should begin and end by following her words closely, beginning with "For years, you have asked: Who is John Galt?" and ending with the idealism of: "The world you desire can be won, it exists, it is real, it is possible, it is yours." In between, we took advantage of many other great lines, though we often had to para-phrase, simplify, condense, or make adjustments for cinematic reasons.

In the novel, for example, Galt's opening line is followed closely by his announcement "This is John Galt speaking." But that was too abrupt for the film. The line has to come as a thunderbolt. To have that effect in the film, we thought the viewers would need a beat after Galt's dramatic takeover from Thompson. They would need time to assimilate the transition, to see the confusion in the studio, to recognize Galt, and to realize that the people in the film are just seeing and hearing him for the first time. So we slowed it down, letting Galt appeal to the sense of despair before announcing himself:

> For years, you have asked: Who is John Galt? You have asked that question in despair and resignation as factories closed, goods became scarce, jobs disappeared. Your lives are becoming more difficult as the life-force of your world is draining away. You have asked that question without expecting an answer. I am here to answer it.
>
> This is John Galt speaking.

Could we have done better with the script? Of course. To pick one of many examples: The final line in the script is not the final line in the novel, where it is followed by Galt's invocation of the strikers' oath. We thought that the poetry of "The world you desire can be won . . ." made for a more rousing call to action, setting up the cheering response of people in the street. But the oath is the single best statement that we reject sacrifice as such, of self to others *and* others to self, when it is voluntary as well as when it is coerced. In retrospect, however, we could have included it in a different way, as indicated in bold:

> . . . In that world, you will not receive alms, nor pity, nor forgiveness of sins -- but honor, respect, and justice. **To win that world, begin by embracing the strikers' oath: "I swear -- by my life and my love of it -- that I will never live for the sake of another man, nor**

```
ask  another  man  to  live  for
mine."
```

```
Don't let the fire go out, spark
by irreplaceable spark, in con-
fusion and despair.
```

```
Be sure of your path. The world
you  desire  can  be  won,  it
exists, it is real, it is pos-
sible, it is yours.
```

In addition, I would have liked to include more of the philo-sophic riches in the novel, such as "the pyramid of ability," the fact that the most talented people, such as those who make new discoveries and invent new products and technologies, contribute the most to oth-ers, while those at the bottom, who are engaged in mere physical labor, benefit the most.

The philosophic and cinematic constraints were so confining that we had to make many hard choices. On the other hand, the script is only one ingredient in the speech. We had the advantage of a talen-ted actor, Kris Polaha, to make the words come alive and resonate with those who see the film. And it is they, the moviegoers, who will have the ultimate verdict. If they see the world differently after leaving the theater or turning off the DVD, we will have succeeded.

CONCLUSION

In both the novel and the movies, the speeches serve to crystal-ize key themes and explain the meaning of the action. *Atlas Shrugged* introduced Ayn Rand's mature philosophy to the world. That philo-sophy is larger than the book or movie, and the speeches, even Galt's speech, give us only an introduction to it. If the speeches have piqued your interest, there is a rich body of thought to explore. It's that under-lying richness of insight that makes *Atlas Shrugged* so powerful and gives it such staying power as a force in our culture.

THE PHILOSOPHY

THE REVOLUTIONARY PHILOSOPHY

OF *ATLAS SHRUGGED*

ROBERT BIDINOTTO

O ne evening after the publication of *The Fountainhead*, Ayn Rand was on the phone, discussing her disappointment over early sales with author Isabel Paterson. Paterson suggested that Rand stop trying to offer her radical ideas in fictional form and instead write a nonfiction treatise. Rand disagreed.

"No, I've presented my case in *The Fountainhead*," she said. "If [people] don't respond, why should I wish to enlighten or help them further? I'm not an altruist."

But Paterson argued that Rand had a *duty* to write nonfiction, because people *needed* her ideas. Rand responded angrily.

"Oh, they do? What if I went on strike? What if *all* the creative minds of the world went on strike?" She added: "*That* would make a good novel."

When she hung up the phone, her husband, Frank O'Connor, said: "It *would* make a good novel."[1]

They talked about it all night—and by morning, she had decided that her next novel would be about "the mind on strike."

In fact, for a long time the working title of the developing story was "The Strike." However, the final title, Atlas Shrugged, concisely symbolizes the book's plot: the rebellion of the unrecognized and often persecuted creative heroes who bear the rest of the world on their shoulders.

As a novelist, Rand chose to create ideal characters. Yet her heroes and heroines defy conventional values. In order to make their motives intelligible and convincing, Rand found that she first had to become a philosopher and to define a new moral ideal.

"My most important job," she wrote in a journal entry, "is the formulation of a rational morality of and for man, of and for his life, of and for this earth." As she noted later, on the eve of publication, "I know that I am challenging the cultural tradition of two and a half thousand years."[2]

Heroes typically reflect prevailing moral codes; and moral codes typically reflect the priorities of their cultures. In primitive societies, where sheer physical survival was the highest priority, tribal codes idealized the strength, prowess, cunning, and bravery of great hunters and warriors. This classical ideal is embodied in the heroes of ancient myths, such as Odysseus in Homer's *Odyssey*, and is still reflected in the action heroes of today's novels, films, and television.

But responding to the suffering so prevalent in ancient societies, religions began to define a different kind of hero. Yearning for a better life after death, their devout followers had to confront worldly temptation, doubt, and persecution. So religious moral codes idealized obedience, self-sacrifice, and unshakable faith. This kind of heroism was embodied by Jesus, and later, by medieval saints and martyrs.

---

1   Barbara Branden, *The Passion of Ayn Rand* (Garden City, NY: Doubleday & Company, 1986).

2   For the latter quote, see *id.*

While classical heroes such as Odysseus were conquering warriors who endured great suffering in order to win fame and fortune, religious heroes such as Jesus were martyrs who renounced worldly pleasures and embraced great suffering, sacrificing themselves to redeem others. Much of human history has been a battle between the champions of these two clashing moral views.

But for the past few hundred years, a new culture has been emerging. The light of reason and science slowly has been pushing back the shadows of superstition and mysticism. Industrial production and international trade have replaced the primitive lifestyles of hunter-gatherer and martial cultures. Blind faith and brute force, once universally hailed as virtues, are completely out of place in a world of computer chips and global financial markets.

And *this* is the world of the Randian hero—a new world demanding a new morality.

In a postscript to *Atlas Shrugged*, Ayn Rand summarized her philosophy this way:

> My philosophy, in essence, is the concept of man as a heroic being, with his own happiness as the moral purpose of his life, with productive achievement as his noblest activity, and reason as his only absolute.

The major theme of *Atlas Shrugged*, embodied in every character, event, and line of dialogue, is: *the role of reason in man's life.*

In Ayn Rand's view, rationality was the essence of the good, and irrationality the essence of evil. So, from the first chapter to the last, the novel depicts the countless ways that human life, well-being, and happiness depend on *thinking*. It shows us what happens whenever somebody assumes the responsibility of using his mind—or whenever he fails to do so.

Now on its face, this doesn't seem very controversial. After all, most people act rationally most of the time: otherwise, they wouldn't survive.

But few people are totally consistent about it. Sometimes, a person exercises exceptional rationality and integrity pursuing his career goals, but then drifts mindlessly and self-destructively in his private life. Or he betrays on Tuesday a course of action he committed himself to on Monday.

Such conflicted lives are filled with frustrations and failures. *Atlas Shrugged* tells us that if left unresolved, conflicts between reason and whim can lead even great men and great nations to destruction.

One of the most dramatic examples in the story is that of Dr. Robert Stadler. A great physicist who is cynical about the prospects for human intelligence in the world, Stadler helps found the State Science Institute, a government body that compels taxpayers to support his scientific research. Because he believes that reason is impotent in the world, he ends up believing that his work must be sustained by brute force. He says to himself: "What can you do when you have to deal with people?"

Even when the institute begins to sponsor work he loathes—such as a book openly attacking reason, written by Dr. Floyd Ferris of the institute's staff—Stadler refuses to repudiate it publicly, for fear of jeopardizing his tax-supported existence. But these contradictions and evasions exact a heavy price on his self-esteem, as Rand describes in this scene:

> When Ferris had gone, Dr. Stadler sat at his desk, his shoulders shrinking together, conscious only of a desperate wish not to be seen by anyone. In the fog of the pain which he would not define, there was also the desperate feeling that no one—no one of those he valued—would ever wish to see him again.

Like the real-life scientists who went to work for the Nazis and Communists, Robert Stadler soon becomes totally dependent on his keepers—and totally corrupted. Though John Galt once had been his most prized student, by the end of the novel Dr. Stadler's voice is among the loudest calling for Galt's execution.

The main reason for moral inconsistencies and betrayals, Ayn Rand believed, is that men have been taught to pursue ideals that are irrational and therefore impractical. Traditional virtues, such as self-sacrifice, faith, and humility, are contrary to the requirements of human life and happiness. They force men into the horrible dilemma of having to choose between virtue and happiness—between morality and life itself.

Hank Rearden is torn in half by such conflicts. He's passion-ately in love with life and happiness—yet he accepts uncritically the con-ventional view that his personal desires are base, even immoral. He regards his love of his work merely as a subjective urge, lacking any nobility or moral significance. This belief leaves him morally defense-less against those who plot to destroy his steel mills.

Similarly, he views his passion for Dagny as animalistic and degrading. This belief leaves him trapped in a loveless marriage, chained to a vicious wife by a gray, empty sense of guilt and moral duty.

The answer to these conflicts, according to Ayn Rand, is a moral code rooted in reason and the requirements of human life, rather than in faith, duty, and selflessness. And because a rational ideal is both moral *and* practical, it ends the need for hypocrisy and inconsistency.

In fact, one of the most startling things readers first notice about Rand's heroes is their complete integrity. Galt, Dagny, and Fran-cisco display consistent loyalty to their principles, not just on import-ant issues, but in the smallest details of everyday life. Holding a moral code rooted in reason and reality allows the Randian hero to act mor-ally *all the time*.

We see this most clearly in the character of John Galt, whose commitment to reason and reality is unbreached. Rand portrays him as a man whom irrationality simply can't tempt—because he can see its destructive consequences too clearly.

Galt's most noticeable trait is his habit of stating bluntly the facts that others prefer not to recognize. Because he doesn't see facts as his enemies, he insists that others face them, too. He refuses even to shield those whom he loves, such as Dagny, from painful truths.

Dagny desperately wants to stay in the valley with Galt—but the thought of giving up her railroad seems unbearable:

> "If only I could stay here and never know what they're doing to the railroad, and never learn when it goes!"
>
> "You'll have to hear about it," said Galt; it was that ruthless tone, peculiarly his, which sounded implacable by being simple, devoid of any emotional value, save the quality of respect for facts. "You'll hear the whole course of the last agony of Taggart Transcontinental. You'll hear about every wreck. You'll hear about every discontinued train. You'll hear about every abandoned line. You'll hear about the collapse of the Taggart Bridge. Nobody stays in this valley except by a full, conscious choice based on a full, conscious knowledge of every fact involved in his decision. Nobody stays here by faking reality in any manner whatever."

The first distinctive feature of the Randian hero, then, is his total, consistent devotion to reason as an absolute. That commitment is the first revolutionary element in Rand's philosophy:

REASON IS MAN'S ONLY VALID
SOURCE OF KNOWLEDGE
AND GUIDE TO ACTION.

By reason, Rand meant thinking applied to the problems of living—practical reason, serving human well-being and happiness. The

Randian hero expresses his commitment to reason and his passion for life through productive work. Which brings us to the second revolutionary element in Ayn Rand's philosophy:

PRODUCTIVE ACHIEVEMENT IS
THE CENTRAL PURPOSE OF LIFE.

Philosopher David Kelley, founder of The Atlas Society, finds Rand's view of productive work central to her moral philosophy: "Ayn Rand's view of productive achievement is the core of her ethic, the point that ties together everything else." That includes her celebration of human reason, her firm commitment to justice, her impassioned defense of capitalism. Rand's exalted view of human potential is based on her concept of Man the Achiever. She saw reason not as mere contemplation detached from the world, but as our means of productive engagement *with* the world.

That's why, as the background for her story of "the mind on strike," she chose not a college campus or literary salon, but the world of industry, focusing on railroads and steel. Here Rand would show the *practical* impact of rationality, or its absence, in the world.

Atlas Shrugged pays tribute to producers and creators of all kinds—to scientists and engineers, artists and musicians, scholars and philosophers. But the main heroes of the story—Dagny, Rearden, Francisco, and Galt—are the children of the Industrial Revolution: self-made businessmen, entrepreneurs, inventors, and financiers. These are the independent souls who—at their own risk, by their own judgment, for their own profit—take the discoveries of scientists and the raw materials of the earth, and transform them for practical uses, as goods and services.

Rand's fullest portrait of the producer is Hank Rearden. Like the great industrialists of the nineteenth century, Rearden is a self-made man of boundless energy, vision, and purpose. All his life, he's maintained a single-tracked devotion to his work. He prides himself on his achievements and the fact that he's let nothing distract or deter him from his path.

He's so vital, so used to confronting and surmounting problems, that he automatically assumes any burden placed before him—even burdens that others deliberately impose upon him. Of all the characters in the novel, Hank Rearden most clearly embodies the symbol of Atlas.

One of the most inspiring illustrations of Rearden's indomitable creative spirit comes at the end of the chapter titled "The Exploiters and the Exploited." An "Equalization of Opportunity" bill has just passed the Legislature. The new law will shatter Rearden's industrial empire, forcing him to sell off his affiliated businesses, including his ore mines.

Trying to go on, Rearden works furiously, past midnight, when suddenly all the pain and anger finally catch up with him:

> He wished he had a friend who could be permitted to see him suffer, without pretense or protection, on whom he could lean for a moment, just to say, "I'm very tired," and find a moment's rest. . . . What was the use? Why had he done it? Why should he ever want to do anything again?

But as his battered mind reflects on all his past achievements, now being ripped from him by the government, it drifts to a current problem—a new bridge for Dagny's railroad—and suddenly a revolutionary structural invention occurs to him:

> In the next moment, he was at his desk, bending over it, with one knee on the seat of the chair, with no time to think of sitting down, he was drawing lines, curves, triangles, columns of calculations, indiscriminately on the blueprints, on the desk blotter, on somebody's letters.
>
> And an hour later, he was calling for a longdistance line, . . . he was saying, "Dagny! That

bridge of ours—throw in the ashcan all the
drawings I sent you, because . . . What? . . .
Oh, that? To hell with that! Never mind the
looters and their laws! Forget it! Dagny, what
do we care? Listen. . . . I've figured out a truss
that will beat anything ever built! Your bridge
will carry four trains at once, stand three
hundred years and cost you less than your
cheapest culvert. I'll send you the drawings in
two days. . . . What? . . . I can't hear you.
Have you caught a cold? . . . What are you
thanking me for, as yet? Wait till I explain it
to you."

One of Ayn Rand's main goals in the novel, according to her
notes, was to show that inventors and industrialists are, as she put it,
"creators in the same sense, with the same heroic virtues, of the same
high *spiritual* order, as the men usually thought of as creators—the
artists."

This, too, challenges conventional morality. Today, philan-
thropists who give away fortunes are regarded as morally superior to
the producers who create them.

But Rand argued that if human life is the standard, then productive work is a major *virtue*—and that anyone who struggles to
achieve despite great obstacles should be regarded as a *hero*.

In the opening pages of *Atlas Shrugged*, Eddie Willers remembers a day in his childhood, when he and Dagny stood near some railroad tracks, talking about what they would do when they grew up.

"You ought to do something great [Eddie
told her] . . . I mean, the two of us together."
"What?" she asked. He said, "I don't know.
That's what we ought to find out. Not just
what you said. Not just business and earning
a living. Things like winning battles, or sav-

ing people out of fires, or climbing mountains." "What for?" she asked. He said, "The
minister said last Sunday that we must
always reach for the best within us. What do
you suppose is the best within us?" "I don't
know." "We'll have to find out." She did not
answer; she was looking away, up the railroad track.

Like Eddie, many people regard business and earning a living
as "worldly" rather than "spiritual" virtues. But Ayn Rand dismissed
any notion of the supernatural—and any division between the moral
and the practical. She described her code as a morality for living on
earth. She didn't view man's need to think and work as a curse upon
human nature—a view that the novel's main villain, James Taggart,
takes to its dead end. He says:

> "I mean, we're only human beings—and
> what's a human being? A weak, ugly, sinful
> creature, born that way, rotten in his bones—
> so humility is the one virtue he ought to prac-
> tice. He ought to spend his life on his knees,
> begging to be forgiven for his dirty existence."

But unlike James Taggart, Ayn Rand believed that in man, mind and
body, consciousness and matter, are indivisible—that, as John Galt puts
it, human nature is not "the battleground . . . between a corpse and a
ghost."

She also rejected the traditional "work ethic," which regards
work as a *duty*—as a punishment for Original Sin. The Randian hero,
by contrast, regards his work as a source of pleasure and profit, of self-
interest and self-expression. Virtue, she declares, isn't its own reward,
or an end in itself. Rather, the ultimate purpose of acting virtuously is
to achieve personal happiness. Man doesn't live in order to work; he
works in order to live.

This is the third revolutionary element in Rand's summary of her philosophy:

A MAN'S OWN HAPPINESS
IS HIS MORAL PURPOSE.

Whatever else they've disagreed about, past views of the moral ideal always shared one conclusion: *they equated heroism with self-sacrifice.* In story and song, tribal groups celebrated the hunter or warrior who dies for his tribe, while religions revered the saint or martyr who dies for his faith.

By contrast, Ayn Rand's stories celebrate the individual who *lives*—not for the sake of others or for some abstraction, but for his own well-being and happiness. Hers was an ethic of enlightened egoism, or what she called *rational self-interest.* "The purpose of morality," says John Galt, "is to teach you, not to suffer and die, but to enjoy yourself and live."

Of all the characters in *Atlas Shrugged*, Francisco d'Anconia most clearly captures this light-hearted joy of living. He leaps from the pages as a creature of pure gaiety and laughter, in love with the fact of his existence.

Francisco is John Galt's closest friend and the first to join him in the strike. While pretending to be a frivolous playboy, he's covertly, ruthlessly destroying his own vast mining empire—and with it, the last resources of his political enemies.

Francisco was one of Ayn Rand's favorite characters:

> In a sense, I created Francisco in the tradition of the Scarlet Pimpernel—or Zorro. . . . Francisco is the philosophical expression—the concretization in a human character—of what I heard in the operetta music I fell in love with in my childhood. Francisco symbolize[s] the enjoyment of life on earth.[3]

---

3 As quoted by Nathaniel Branden in *Judgment Day* (Boston: Houghton-Mifflin, 1989).

Easily the most romantic figure Rand ever invented, Francisco d'Anconia is also her most compelling portrait of the practical man of action. Serenely confident and supremely capable, Francisco confronts any obstacle or challenge as if it were merely another opportunity to exercise his enormous talents. And though the strike ultimately costs him both his family fortune and the woman he loves, he remains untouched by any hint of tragedy.

Consider the scene of Dagny's final night in the valley, where Francisco pours a toast for her, Galt, and himself. Suddenly he realizes that the woman he has waited for, for twelve lonely years, has fallen in love with his best friend, John Galt. Imagine how most men might react to such a stunning realization—but observe how Francisco responds:

> Francisco's hand stopped. For a long moment, he was seeing nothing but Galt's face. Then his eyes moved to hers. He put the bottle down and he did not step back, but it was as if his glance drew back to a wide range, to include them both.
>
> "But of course," he said. . . .
>
> . . . "It could not have been otherwise. It is as it had—and ought—to be. It was set then, twelve years ago." He looked at Galt and chuckled softly. "And you say that it's *I* who've taken the hardest beating?"
>
> . . . He picked up the two silver goblets, looked down at them for the pause of an instant, then extended one to Dagny, the other to Galt.
>
> "Take it," he said. "You've earned it—and it wasn't chance."

In every way, Francisco represents the conventional morality stood on its head. Where traditional codes uphold meekness, mercy, and selflessness, he's boldly self-assured, implacably just, and passionately assertive.

He's also the antithesis of the public image he deliberately adopts—the irresponsible hedonist. A man of iron determination, Francisco thinks, plans, and acts long-range. When Dagny asks him, "What's the most depraved kind of human being?" Francisco answers: "The man without a purpose."

"He flew through the days . . . like a rocket," Rand wrote, "but if one stopped him in mid-flight, he could always name the purpose of his every random moment. Two things were impossible to him: to stand still or to move aimlessly."

This brings us to an aspect of Rand's philosophy that still confuses many people. She advocated a morality she called "rational self-interest." Today, "self-interest" has come to mean: blindly indulging your desires and whims—doing whatever you *feel* like doing—sacrificing others to benefit yourself. So some people believe that Rand's philosophy of self-interest must amount to hedonism—and that the only moral alternative to such a self-indulgent outlook is to selflessly suppress and sacrifice your personal desires.

But as a champion of reason, Rand abhorred the mindless "selfishness" of the hedonist, the materialist, and the criminal. She rejected *both* self-indulgence *and* self-sacrifice as false alternatives, equally irrational and self-destructive. Indulging whims, she argued, won't bring happiness, but only frustration, misery, and ruin.

Early in the novel, we see James Taggart after he's spent the night with a cheap, brainless society girl, Betty Pope. In the morning, through the haze of a hangover, Taggart looks at Betty's clothes scattered around his room, and hears her gargling through the open door of the bathroom.

> Why do I do those things?—he thought, remembering last night. But it was too much trouble to look for an answer. . . .

> The nature of their relationship had . . . no
> passion in it, no desire, no actual pleasure,
> not even a sense of shame. To them, the act
> of sex was neither joy nor sin. It meant noth-
> ing. They had heard that men and women
> were supposed to sleep together, so they did.

Contrast this mindless, empty relationship with the passionate romances of the novel's heroes. Rand meant for us to understand that romantic pleasure—like any other human value—arises from *full consciousness*. Hers is a morality of *rational* self-interest—of self-interest governed by reason, not whims.

But if reason is our only means of successfully dealing with reality, and if irrationality leads to destruction, what explains the widespread presence of irrationality in the world? Why do evil people, like James Taggart, so often seem to triumph?

In one of her most important insights, Ayn Rand pointed out that no evil person or irrational scheme can possibly succeed—*unless they're assisted and supported by rational people*. Evil is basically irrational and self-destructive. For it to survive and succeed, it depends on the aid and support of its victims—the good and the rational.

The novel gives us many examples. Rearden's family treats him cruelly—but only because he continues to support them financially. James Taggart, a vicious incompetent, uses his position as head of the railroad to thwart Dagny's efforts and destroy her business allies—but only because she continues to run the railroad for him, sustaining him in that position of power. The fascist gang in Washington uses its power to loot businesses—but only because businessmen like Dagny and Rearden continue to produce and provide them the loot.

But *why* do the victims of evil tolerate such exploitation? Rand blamed *the moral code of self-sacrifice*. It damns people as greedy and selfish for pursuing their own happiness and makes them feel ashamed of their personal goals, achievements, and wealth. Parasites and power-seekers exploit such guilty feelings in order to manipulate, control, and loot their victims.

For example, Dr. Floyd Ferris threatens to expose Rearden's extramarital affair with Dagny—unless Rearden signs away to the government all rights to his invention, Rearden Metal.

> [Ferris:] "We knew that no form of personal injury would ever make you give in. . . . This will not hurt you at all. It will only hurt Miss Taggart. . . ."
>
> [Rearden:] "But all your calculations rest on the fact that Miss Taggart is a virtuous woman, not the slut you're going to call her."
>
> "Yes, of course," said Dr. Ferris. . . .
>
> "If our relationship were the depravity you're going to proclaim it to be, you'd have no way to harm us."
>
> "No."
>
> "We'd be outside your power."
>
> "Actually—yes."

Yet still accepting the idea that publicizing their affair would expose Dagny to shame, Rearden gives in to the blackmail scheme. The extortion works only because he had accepted the morality that condemns his affair as base and selfish. If instead he had viewed their relationship with unconflicted moral *pride*, he'd have been immune to any threat of exposure. But the moral code of dutiful self-sacrifice disarms him.

To defeat such evils, Rand declared, the victims had to reject the moral code that damns *them* as evil. This philosophical insight provided the central idea for her plot: the strike of the men of reason against the society that condemns, sacrifices, and plunders them. In *Atlas Shrugged*, she allows John Galt to speak for her:

> It is the victims who made injustice possible.
> It is the men of reason who made it possible
> for the rule of the brute to work. . . . But
> this time—*it will not last*. The victims are on
> strike. We are on strike against martyrdom—
> and against the moral code that demands it.
> We are on strike against those who believe
> that one man must exist for the sake of
> another.

Ayn Rand's morality of rational self-interest regards *each individual's life and happiness as an end in itself.* Its social corollary is that

> NO INDIVIDUAL MAY BE FORCED
> AGAINST HIS WILL
> TO SERVE AS A MEANS TO THE ENDS OF OTHERS.

This idea lies at the base of the political ideas in *Atlas Shrugged*.

When, as a girl in Russia, she first heard the Communist slogan that the individual should live for the state, Ayn Rand knew *this* was the principle that was making all the other Soviet horrors possible. Later, thinking of Cyrus, her childhood hero, she told Barbara Branden: "I saw in that slogan the vision of Cyrus on a sacrificial altar, crucified in the name of mediocrity."

But *why* do people think it's good to sacrifice individuals for the sake of the group? For one thing, they believe that human interests unavoidably must clash, so that one person's gain is another person's loss. This implies that someone's interests must be sacrificed, if another's are to be furthered—that the individual must be sacrificed, if the group is to prosper.

This combative view of society seemed perfectly sensible to our tribal and feudal ancestors. In those days, life's necessities were in short supply, and the strong grew wealthy by plundering the weak.

That's why religions preached humility and self-sacrifice: by getting strong individuals to curb their appetites, it seemed that society as a whole might be better off.

But the Industrial Revolution exploded that myth. By using his reason, man began to transform unused raw materials into unlimited abundance. As a producer, he did not gain at the expense of others, but instead generated for himself wealth that never before existed. He was no longer a parasite or predator, like James Taggart, but instead, a true *creator*, like Hank Rearden.

And this new wealth spread rapidly throughout society, by means of trade. People exchanged goods and services they produced for those produced by others. In trading, each person swapped what he valued *less* for things he wanted *more*. The free economy wasn't a "zero-sum game," with winners and losers. Through production and peaceful trade, everyone benefited, and no one lost.

Trade proves that there are no necessary conflicts of interest among people. In fact, there's a natural *harmony of interests*—at least, among those people who deal with each other rationally and voluntarily: by production and exchange, rather than by plunder and force.

Consider the scene in which Dagny tells Rearden she needs a large quantity of Rearden Metal faster than originally agreed. He demands an additional $20 per ton.

> "Pretty steep, Hank. Is that the best price you can give me?"

> "No. But that's the one I'm going to get. I could ask twice that and you'd pay it."

> "Yes, I would. And you could. But you won't."

> "Why won't I?"

> "Because you need to have the Rio Norte Line built. It's your first showcase for Rearden Metal."

He chuckled. "That's right. I like to deal with somebody who has no illusions about getting favors." . . .

". . . So you think it's right that I should squeeze every penny of profit I can, out of your emergency?"

"I'm not a moocher, Hank."

All proper social relationships, Rand said, must be based on reason, not force. To ensure this, the *initiation of force* must be banned in society. And not just brute force, but all variations of it—such as fraud and threats of force. The only proper use of force is defensive or retaliatory against the person who started its use.

Not even the government is morally entitled to initiate force, Ayn Rand argued. Governments should be limited to using only defensive force to protect people's rights—that and nothing else.

This means there should be no laws restricting any peaceful, voluntary activities: no laws interfering with economic or personal relationships; no limits on production or trade; no seizures of honestly acquired private property; and no deprivations of human liberty, except in retaliation for a crime.

Through reason and freedom, an individual can achieve personal happiness and reach his full, productive, heroic potential. This, in a nutshell, is the revolutionary philosophy Ayn Rand introduced in *Atlas Shrugged*. This was her new moral ideal for a new age.

AN OUTLINE
OF GALT'S SPEECH

DAVID KELLEY

In *Atlas Shrugged*, the hero, John Galt, makes a radio speech to the nation revealing the strike of the producers and explaining its rationale. The speech resolves the philosophical mystery of the plot: Why are the most productive people leaving their work and disappearing from society? As such, it provides a comprehensive introduction to Ayn Rand's philosophy, though one that is tailored to the events and characters of the novel. In later works, Rand presented specific elements of her philosophy in nonfiction terms.

Ayn Rand regarded Galt's speech as the shortest summary of her philosophy, which she called Objectivism. "I knew it was going to be the hardest chapter in the book," she told an interviewer in 1961. "I underestimated. I thought, with a feeling of dread, that it would take at least three months. Well, it took two years." Rand began outlining the speech on July 29, 1953; it was not completed until October 13, 1955.

Her biggest challenge was not the speech's philosophical content but its literary requirements. In a novel, she could not present her ideas in the form of a dry, systematic treatise; she had to state them dramatically, in the form of a revolutionary leader's manifesto and challenge to a corrupt society.

"I started by making an outline of the issues to be covered," Rand explained. "I originally began the theoretical presentation with metaphysics, starting with 'existence exists,' going from metaphysics to epistemology, then planning to go to morality. After writing quite a few pages, I had to stop because I knew it was absolutely wrong. That is the logical order in non-fiction, but you can't do it in fiction. The speech had to start by presenting the morality, which is the real theme of the book, and where Galt would have to begin his explanation to the world. So I had to rewrite the whole thing."

Though the speech is written as a single, continuous presentation, it can be divided into three sections. In the first, Galt presents the moral code of reason and individualism (the "morality of life") that the producers embrace. In the second, he explains and attacks the opposite moral code of mysticism, sacrifice, and collectivism (the "morality of death"), showing how it has always been used to exploit the producers. In the third section, he explains the strategy of the strike—the withdrawal of "the sanction of the victim"—and urges his listeners to reexamine their moral assumptions. This section also presents the political ideals that follow from the moral code of rational individualism.

I have prepared this outline as an aid to those who wish to understand the speech, whether as a statement of Rand's philosophical ideas or as a literary element in her novel. The outline breaks the three sections into subsections where each main point that Galt makes is stated in essential terms and in such a way as to indicate the logical flow of his speech. Reading this outline is no substitute for reading the speech itself, but it will help you keep the full context in mind as you study each element.

Galt's speech can be found in part 3, chapter 7 of *Atlas Shrugged* ("This is John Galt Speaking"). It was also reproduced in Ayn

Rand's *For the New Intellectual.* To connect this outline with the text of the speech, I have begun each subsection of the outline with the opening words, in italics, of the first paragraph it relates to in the text. (Page numbers could not be used for this purpose since they vary among the many printings of these books.)

I. The Morality of Life
   A. The Moral Crisis
      "You have heard it said that this is an age of moral crisis."
      1. The moral crisis was brought about by the doctrine of sacrifice.
      2. Galt has led a strike to protest that doctrine and to remove the men of justice, independence, reason, wealth, and self-esteem—the men of the mind.
      3. The crisis demands the discovery of a proper morality.
   B. The Standard and Purpose of Morality
      "You have heard no concepts of morality . . ."
      1. The essence of previous moral codes is to demand that you surrender your mind and your life to the whims of God or society.
      2. The mind is man's basic means of survival.
      3. Because thinking is volitional, man needs a conscious code of values.
      4. For any living organism, its life is its fundamental value, since existence or non-existence is its fundamental alternative.
      5. To maintain its life, any organism must act in accordance with its means of survival. For man, this means living by the exercise of his mind.
      6. Man's life—the life of man qua rational being—is the proper *standard* of value. Your own life—and happiness as its emotional concomitant—is the *purpose* of morality.
      7. You can choose not to live, you can choose not to think, but you cannot avoid the consequences of such

choices—except by trying to make others pay for your defaults.

C. The Nature of Reason

"*We, the men of the mind, are now on strike against you. . . .*"

1. All thinking rests on the axioms that reality exists, that we are aware of it, and that things are what they are. A is A.

2. Reason is the faculty that integrates the material provided by man's senses in accordance with logic.

3. The individual must initiate and direct his own capacity for reason and act on the basis of his own rational judgment.

4. "A rational process is a moral process." Our free will consists in the choice to think or not to think. Thinking is the basic moral virtue; evasion is the basic vice.

D. The Content of a Rational Moral Code

"*My morality, the morality of reason . . .*"

1. The morality of reason follows from the axiom that existence exists and the choice to live.

2. Reason, purpose, and self-esteem are cardinal values.

3. These values imply and require the virtues of rationality, independence, integrity, honesty, justice, productiveness, and pride.

4. But virtue is not its own reward. "*Life* is the reward of virtue—and happiness is the goal and the reward of life."

5. Pleasure and pain, joy and suffering, are the emotional forms in which we experience values. But emotions are governed by what we choose to value.

6. True happiness is "a state of non-contradictory joy," and is thus possible only to those who pursue rational values.

7. There are "no conflicts of interest among rational men."

8. The proper means of interaction with others is trade.

9. The initiation of physical force is evil; it prevents the victim from acting on the basis of his mind. Force may be used only in retaliation and only against those who start its use.

II. The Morality of Death

   A. Transition

     "In the name of all the producers who had kept you alive . . ."

     1. The producers will no longer work under threat of coercion.

     2. The producers are motivated by positive values—life, happiness, achievement. Their exploiters are motivated by negatives—death, misery, destruction.

     3. Opposed to the morality of life is the morality of death, which demands that man atone for the guilt of being human by sacrificing his mind, values, and happiness.

   B. The Doctrine of Original Sin

     "The name of this monstrous absurdity is Original Sin."

     1. The motive of the doctrine of original sin is to instill guilt and thus nullify man's right to question moral commands.

     2. Moral concepts like sin apply only to voluntary action. That which is outside the possibility of choice is outside the province of morality. In holding that man is innately evil, the doctrine of original sin negates morality.

     3. The doctrine says that man is evil because he possesses reason, knowledge, morality, productiveness, creativity, the capacity for sexual pleasure, and the capacity for joy —all the cardinal values of his existence.

   C. The Mind/Body Dichotomy

     "No, they say, they do not preach that man is evil. . . ."

     1. The dichotomy holds that soul and body have incompatible natures, needs, and aims, and that the good of the soul requires the negation of the body.

    2. The dichotomy presupposes the negation of reason, leaving man to choose between guidance by physical instincts and guidance by mystic emotions.

    3. The mystics of spirit substitute revelation for reason; they demand that the individual surrender his mind and self-interest to the will of God.

    4. The mystics of muscle substitute reflexes for reason; they demand that the individual surrender his mind and self-interest to the will of society.

    5. Both varieties of mystics preach the same moral doctrine: self-sacrifice.

D. The Doctrine of Sacrifice

"Whoever is now within reach of my voice . . ."

    1. "A sacrifice is the surrender of a value"—of a higher value to a lower one, or of the good to the evil.

    2. The code is impossible to practice because it would lead to death, and thus moral perfection is impossible to man.

    3. The doctrine of sacrifice cannot provide man with an interest in being good.

    4. Since man is in fact an indivisible unity of matter and consciousness, the sacrifice of "merely" material values necessarily means the sacrifice of spiritual ones.

    5. The self is the mind, and the most selfish act is the exercise of one's independent judgment. In attacking selfishness, the doctrine of sacrifice seeks to make you surrender your mind.

    6. The doctrine of sacrifice commands that you act for the good of others but provides no standard of the good. And it requires only that you intend to benefit others, not that you succeed.

    7. The doctrine of sacrifice makes you the servant and others your masters—and adds insult to injury by saying you should find happiness through sacrifice.

E. Sacrifice and the Unearned

"You who have no standard of self-esteem . . ."

1. If you must act to benefit others, why is it acceptable for others to accept such benefits? Because they did not earn them. At its core, the doctrine of sacrifice is a doctrine that seeks the unearned.

2. Lack of value gives one a claim upon those who possess value. The doctrine elevates failure, weakness, need, incompetence, suffering, vice, and irrationality and regards them as moral claims on success, strength, wealth, ability, joy, virtue, and rationality.

3. On this inversion of values, one sacrifices morality and self-esteem and becomes both a victim and a parasite, with no standard of how much sacrifice is enough.

4. In the spiritual realm, the doctrine of the unearned commands unconditional love, love based on need rather than value, love for those who do not deserve it—because they do not deserve it.

F. Mysticism as the Basis for the Unearned

"The mystics of both schools, who preach the creed . . ."

1. The mystics exploit your fear of relying on your mind by positing a higher form of knowledge: supernatural (the "mystics of spirit") or skeptical (the "mystics of muscle").

2. They claim to perceive a reality exempt from the law of identity, in order to make their wishes—their whims—absolutes.

3. "There is no honest revolt against reason." The motive is always to indulge one's emotions, and the effect is always to subvert one's ability to grasp reality.

4. The mystics seek to evade the law of causality—which is "the law of identity applied to action"—in order to gain values without effort and justify their demand for unearned love, admiration, and wealth.

5. Since there is no actual escape from identity and causality, from the need to think and produce in order to create values, the producers are expected to pay for the default of the irrational.

G. The Modern Mystics of Muscle

   "Just as your mystics of spirit invented their heaven . . ."

1. The modern mystics of muscle attack reason through skepticism, denying the validity of the axioms of reason.

2. Axioms are statements that identify the bases of knowledge. These bases include or imply that things exist and are what they are, that they act according to their natures, that facts are absolute, and that sense-perception is valid.

3. In denying these truths, the mystics of muscle would reduce man's consciousness to the level of a baby or a primitive tribe.

4. While the mystics of spirit claim that faith is superior to reason, the mystics of muscle claim that reason is merely faith and substitute collective opinion for objective knowledge. They even deny the existence of the mind.

5. Their motive is to reverse cause and effect, to demand goods without producing them, to control the producers, and to redistribute their wealth.

H. The Psychology of the Mystics

   "Did you wonder what is wrong with the world?"

1. The mystics of muscle and of spirit have had the same motive throughout history: to undercut your mind and to rule you by force.

2. Having surrendered their own judgment to avoid clashes with others, they regard the judgments of others as a power superior to reason, believing that others have a mysterious link with reality.

3. To control reality, they must therefore control others, seeking obedience at all costs. Their goal is to control the consciousness of others as a means of getting control over reality.

4. Death is the only state that satisfies the mystics' desire for exemption from identity and causality. Poverty, suffering, destruction, and death are the consequences of their moral code—and the real motive of the code. Mystics have defaulted on the responsibility to think, act, and produce; they feel envious hatred toward, and wish to destroy, those who have not defaulted.

III. Return to Reason and Freedom

  A. The Sanction of the Victim Withdrawn

    "We, who were the living buffers between you and the nature of your creed . . ."

    1. Galt describes how he grasped the nature of the morality of death—and what to do about it.

    2. Since evil is irrational, it can succeed only with the consent and aid of the rational. The morality of death is perpetuated by the sanction of its victims—the men of reason and ability. The strike is the withdrawal of that sanction.

    3. The morality of death counts on the producers to think and produce, while denying them the honor they deserve and the freedom they require. Its strategy is to induce moral guilt in the men of reason and ability. The strikers refuse to accept guilt for their ability.

    4. Galt is doing by conscious design what men of ability had done throughout the ages: withdrawing their talents from the world. He is teaching the producers their own value.

    5. Without the victims whom Galt has withdrawn, the morality of death and those who embrace it will collapse of their own irrationality.

B. Take an Inventory of Your Mind

"But to those of you who still retain a remnant of the dignity and will to love one's life . . ."

1. If you retain the wish to live, you must examine your values and your life in order to avert self-destruction.

2. Altruism creates a clash between the moral and the practical by setting the standards of morality in opposition to the requirements of living. It thus deprives you of practical guidance, moral certainty, and the capacity for happiness, dignity, and self-esteem.

3. There are moral absolutes, and moral judgment is a necessity. "In any compromise between good and evil, it is only evil that can profit."

4. It is absurd to believe, as political conservatives do, that collectivism is based on reason and science while freedom, production, and trade must be accepted on faith. This absurdity is a rationalization to avoid questioning the moral code of self-sacrifice.

5. People refuse to question that code because their self-esteem is tied to it. As a being with free will, man, by nature, needs self-esteem and moral self-approval; but men have tied their self-esteem to a morality that undercuts it.

6. Their fear and guilt spring from the awareness of having willfully abandoned reason and having refused to think for themselves.

7. The myths of paradise reflect the spirit of childhood: the joyous, fearless "independence of a rational consciousness facing an open universe." It is not too late to begin again:

   a. Accept the fact that your mind works by choice, not automatically, and that your life depends on choosing to think.

    b. Learn to trust your mind and to act by your own independent reason, not on the basis of authority.

    c. Seek moral perfection in the unbreached exercise of rationality, and learn to distinguish errors of knowledge from moral evil.

    d. Choose happiness as your moral purpose and give it your full commitment.

    e. Learn to value yourself by rejecting humility as a virtue and seeking pride.

    f. Give help to others when deserved, but not on the basis of need alone or when demanded as a right.

8. In betraying these requirements of life and happiness, you have sacrificed your virtues to your vices within your soul. In society, you have sacrificed the best men to the worst.

C. A Society of Traders

"It was the three of us who started what I am now completing."

1. But now the best men have refused to submit to the rule of force and brutality. The strikers are avenging the spirit of America.

2. America was founded on reason and individualism, "on the inviolate supremacy of man's right to exist and achieve." It cannot survive on an altruist moral basis.

3. The strike will end only when the morality of sacrifice is abandoned and the country can be rebuilt on the moral premise that each individual is an end in himself.

4. Individual rights are not gifts from God or society. They are conditions required by man's nature for his proper survival.

5. Without property rights, individuals could not translate their other rights into reality. All property and wealth are created by man's mind and labor, and they would

cease to exist without the due recognition of their source: individual intelligence.

6. The only proper purpose of government is to protect rights. A government's only proper functions are: the police; the armed forces; and the courts, to settle disputes by objective law. Government must not initiate force against people.

7. Productive men cannot function long-range if they are subject to the capricious edicts of rulers.

8. In a society of trade, there is no conflict of interests among men at different levels in the pyramid of ability. The most talented people, such as those who make new discoveries and invent new products and technologies, contribute the most to others; while those at the bottom, who are engaged in mere physical labor, benefit the most.

9. Producers require freedom to act on their minds, take risks, trade with others, and earn and keep their profits.

10. In rejecting this demand as unfair, you have created instead a society of brutality and plunder, in which gangs battle for control of the government and the power to extort wealth.

D. Call to Action

"But it is not to him that I wish to speak."

1. "Stop supporting your own destroyers." Do not sanction them, and do not try to live on their terms.

2. Do not contribute your achievements to them. When they force you, obey, but do not volunteer anything. Do not help criminals pretend that they are your benefactors.

3. In your own mind and life, practice the morality of life. "You have no chance to win on the Morality of Death."

4. When the looters' state collapses, the producers will return, and those who wish to live by our code can rejoin us.

5. Our political system will be based on the moral premise that no one may obtain values by physical force. Each must live by his own rational judgment.

6. In that world you may live without fear, among people who are responsible and reliable. It will be a just world, where your virtues will be rewarded and mutual respect among people will be possible.

7. Fight for this world, "in the name of the best within you." You will win when you are ready to pronounce this oath: "I swear—by my life and my love of it—that I will never live for the sake of another man, nor ask another man to live for mine."

THE CAPITALIST IDEAL
The Moral Vision of *Atlas Shrugged*

DAVID KELLEY

I n 1917, Bolsheviks under Lenin seized control of Russia in the famous October revolution, ending a short-lived experiment with constitutional democracy and replacing it with a one-party socialist state. As the revolution swirled through the streets of St. Petersberg, a girl of 12 watched many of the events from the balcony of her family's house. That girl was Alyssa Rosenbaum, who ultimately left Russia for America and became the writer we know as Ayn Rand. In 1957, she published her final and greatest novel, *Atlas Shrugged*.

Atlas Shrugged is a revolutionary work, but the revolution it represents is diametrically opposed to the one its author lived through as a youth. In the eight years before she left the Soviet Union in 1925, Rand lived through the economic chaos and desperate poverty communism caused, as the government nationalized businesses and expropriated private wealth. Her father was a pharmacist, and Rand was in the shop when soldiers arrived to close the business and seize the property, depriving the family of work, property, and income. In the years before she left, she lived through the tyranny of statism, as the communists used every means to expand their power—including secret police, terror tactics, and executing enemies or shipping them to Siberia. Under the new communist regime, more and more of private life was politicized, including speech, ideas, and education.

Rand was appalled by this system. She was appalled not merely by its visible effects on herself and the people she knew. She was appalled by the underlying ideology of communism, especially the ideas of moral collectivism that made communism possible and were used to justify it as a noble ideal. Even as a child, she knew there was something horribly wrong in the idea of sacrificing the individual to the collective, breaking eggs to make an omelet.

Her first published novel, *We the Living*, offers a portrait of Russia in those years and of the crushing effects of communism on people of ability, ambition, and independent spirit. But *Atlas* is her fullest and deepest portrayal of the issues involved. It goes far beyond the specifics of any particular type of system—communist, fascist, communitarian, whatever—to deal with the essence of collectivism.

And, more importantly, to present the essence of individualism, including the capitalism system of economic freedom. What she meant by capitalism is not the mixed economy characteristic of all the industrialized countries, in which the government consumes a third or more of all production and heavily regulates the rest. She meant laissez-faire, "with a separation of state and economics, in the same way and for the same reasons as the separation of state and church." The function of government is solely to protect individual rights, including property rights. When it redistributes wealth, nationalizes industries, or regulates voluntary transactions among consenting adults, it commits the moral fallacy of socialism, the fallacy of treating the individual as a means to the collective good.

Rand's great achievement was to offer a vision of capitalism as a moral ideal. Her characters illustrate the virtues of rationality, production, and trade—and the vices of parasitism and power. The narrative dramatizes the struggle of producers against parasites and predators, and traces the consequences of that struggle across a whole society. And the meaning of these events is put into words, in speeches by various characters that lay out a new philosophy and moral code of individualism. In its characters, its plot and its philosophical themes, *Atlas* is about a new revolution, a capitalist revolution. It is truly the capitalist manifesto.

I want to explain a little more fully what I mean by the novel's revolutionary character. I'll begin with the narrative, which tells the story of a kind of revolution, and then turn to the core ideas of the book.

THE STORY

As a novel, *Atlas* has the form of a mystery story. We follow two major characters, Dagny Taggart and Hank Rearden, as they try to find answers to the puzzles of their world. Dagny is the vice president of operations of Taggart Transcontinental, the largest railroad in the United States. Rearden is the head of a steel-manufacturing company that he started from scratch and built into the best-run, most profitable company in the industry. As the story opens, Rearden has just started producing a new alloy he invented, Rearden Metal, and Dagny is his first customer. She wants to have rails of the metal to replace a branch line in Colorado, where many new factories have located and need better transportation for their products.

Dagny and Rearden are surrounded by people who put obstacles in their way. Dagny's brother James is the president of the railroad; he is afraid to rely on his own business judgment, and he fears and resents those who trust theirs. He is more of a political type. He spends most of his time on public relations and scheming to use political connections to get government subsidies and regulations that harm competing railroads. Orren Boyle, head of a steel company competing with Rearden, is a crony of James Taggart's and operates the same way. He never delivers steel on time or makes a profit, but he has great press and political connections.

There's also Wesley Mouch, Rearden's "man in Washington," who sells Rearden out at a key moment by going along with a kind of antitrust law aimed at Rearden. And there's the State Science Institute, whose Machiavellian, power-hungry "top co-ordinator" attacks Rearden Metal, without evidence, as a possible danger to the public.

Over and above the obstacles that villains like these place in the way of Dagny, Rearden, and other genuine producers, there is something palpably wrong with the world. The society seems to be in some sort of decline. Buildings and machinery are in disrepair, things break and don't get fixed, businesses close or cut back, competent people are hard to find. Economically it seems like a recession, but there's a recession of the spirit, too, a mood of despair, futility, and resignation captured in what has become a popular expression: "Who is John Galt?" An odd thing about this state of affairs is that a number of highly talented people seem to be disappearing, including some prominent achievers at the peak of their success.

Working against seemingly impossible odds, Dagny succeeds in completing her railroad's Colorado branch line, which she has named the John Galt Line in defiance of the general mood of despair. Rearden works closely with her—it's the first showcase of his metal—and they soon become lovers. Rand's description of the first run of the John Galt Line is one of the most vivid and powerful things she ever wrote: vivid in describing the train's motion as it hurtles through the mountainous terrain; powerful in the inner reflections Dagny has about the personal meaning of the experience, as a celebration of her achievement.

Unfortunately, the triumph is short-lived. The government's control over the economy has been growing. The public resents the business boom in Colorado and is clamoring for a special tax on the state and for equal train service in all states. Now that the worth of Rearden Metal has been proven and demand for it is has skyrocketed, the government begins regulating how much Rearden can sell, and to whom. The only bright spot in the increasingly grim situation is that Dagny and Rearden find a motor in an abandoned factory, a motor that appears to have been a technological breakthrough. But what is it doing in a junk heap? And what happened to the genius who invented it?

As Dagny tries to solve that mystery by searching for the inventor, she is increasingly convinced that the disappearances of so many productive people must be some kind of organized plot.

It is, as Dagny eventually discovers. Led by the man who invented the motor, the best producers are engaged in a strike: to withdraw their talent, work, and ability to create wealth from a society that dishonors their work even as it expropriates what they have produced. And they have set a condition for their return: the recognition of their right to produce and trade freely, without state interference. In effect, they are demanding a capitalist revolution. Their leader, John Galt, has issued the call: Capitalists of the world, unite! You have nothing to lose but your chains.

The moral philosophy embodied in the strike can be broken down into three broad themes. *Atlas Shrugged* actually conveys a multitude of ideas that are dramatized by the events and explained in a long speech—a radio address—in which Galt tells the world what the strike has been about. But these three are the deepest, most essential ones, the ones that really make the novel an intellectual revolution as well as an exciting story. If you get these, you get the book. They are:

- The glory of production
- The morality of self-interest
- The justice of trade

THE GLORY OF PRODUCTION

At the beginning of *Atlas Shrugged*, Eddie Willers recalls a childhood conversation with Dagny Taggart.

> "You ought to do something great . . . I mean, the two of us together." "What?" she asked. He said, "I don't know. That's what we ought to find out. Not just what you said. Not just business and earning a living. Things

like winning battles, or saving people out of
fires, or climbing mountains. . . . The minister said last Sunday that we must always reach
for the best within us. What do you suppose
is the best within us?"

By the end of the novel, Eddie knows the answer to that question, and so do we. *Atlas Shrugged* is a novel about producers, specifically business producers, and it celebrates them as heroes. Rand's first
theme is that production is good. It is good not only because the
things we produce support our lives, and provide comfort and security;
it is good because the activity of production is an activity of creative
achievement, adding value to our world through the exercise of intelligence and effort. Rand sees production in moral as well as economic
terms, as an expression of the best within us.

Hank Rearden is the character who provides the full template
for the virtues of the producers. He is truly the *Atlas* of the novel's
title, the giant who supports the world by creating wealth.

He came from utter poverty. He began working in the Minnesota iron ore mines at age 14. He worked, learned, and saved, until
he bought the mines, then an abandoned steel plant, and then coal
mines, from which he built the most successful steel company in the
business. And then he spent ten years of research and experimentation
to invent a new metal alloy much better than steel.

His character as a producer is shown in countless ways throughout the novel. Rearden is a man of purpose and vision, with the self-
generated will to pursue the vision in reality. When the first heat of
Rearden Metal is poured, he thinks back to what kept him going
through the exhausting process of trial and error:

the one thought held immovably across a
span of ten years, under everything he did
and everything he saw, the thought held in
his mind when he looked at the buildings of
a city, at the track of a railroad, at the light in

the windows of a distant farmhouse, at the
knife in the hands of a beautiful woman cutting a piece of fruit at a banquet, the thought
of a metal alloy that would do more than
steel had ever done, a metal that would be to
steel what steel had been to iron.

Rearden is a man who takes responsibility for his decisions and
actions, not just in business but in every area of life. He is his own
harshest judge and taskmaster. At the root of his character, infusing all
his other traits, is an absolute commitment to objectivity, to accepting
facts as facts without evasion or wishful thinking. He not only has a
brilliant, creative mind in the sense of intelligence and knowledge, he
is committed to using his mind to the fullest, to understanding the
world as it is, to finding truth and speaking it honestly. In other words,
he not only has a highly developed capacity for reason, he possesses the
moral virtue of rationality.

Finally, Rearden is a man of pride, in himself and his accom-
plishments. In one of the first efforts of the looters to expropriate
Rearden Metal, the State Science Institute attempts to buy the rights to
Rearden Metal and take it off the market. Rearden refuses. When a
Dr. Potter from the institute asks why he wants to make his gains over
years, squeezing out a profit margin penny by penny, rather than accept
a government check now, Rearden says, "Because it's mine. Do you
understand the word?" In the final lines of the scene, Potter again asks
Rearden why he is refusing. "It's because Rearden Metal is *good*,"
Rearden says.

One of the things that Rand conveys about production—over
and over again, in many different forms—is that the source of material
achievements and wealth lies in the spirit of the producers. Early in the
novel, we hear Dagny reflecting:

Motive power—thought Dagny, looking up at
the Taggart Building in the twilight—was its
first need; motive power, to keep that

building standing; movement, to keep it
immovable. It did not rest on piles driven
into granite; it rested on engines that rolled
across a continent.

And what do those engines rest on? Riding in the locomotive on the
first run of the John Galt Line, Dagny walks into the engine room:

They are alive, she thought, because they are
the physical shape of the action of a living
power—of the mind that had been able to
grasp the whole of this complexity, to set its
purpose, to give it form.

They are alive, she thought, but their soul
operates them by remote control. Their soul
is in every man who has the capacity to equal
this achievement. Should the soul vanish
from the earth, the motors would stop,
because that is the power which keeps them
going . . . the power of a living mind—the
power of thought and choice and purpose."

Rand is of course speaking metaphorically here, but the metaphor is a powerful one that resonates throughout the novel, and stands
for a truth that is not a metaphor: Material production has a spiritual
core.

Conversely, when the spirit is gone, machines, buildings, roads
—all the products of industrial production—reduce to inert matter.
And, quickly enough, they rust, decay, break down, fall apart, and
revert to natural elements. In Aristotle's sense of soul as the animating
principle of a living thing, human intelligence is the soul of the
machine. In portraying a society in decline, Atlas has many scenes that
illustrate the point. For example, when Dagny and Rearden find the
abandoned factory, the countryside they pass through is in deep industrial decline. People are in fact living in pre-industrial conditions: no

electricity, few paved roads, no travel to the next town, hand plows to till the fields. The inhabitants are using the relics and debris of industry for the accidental purposes permitted by their physical shapes: telegraph wire to hang laundry, engine cylinders as flower pots, etc. This is the image of what happens when the mental/spiritual source of industry—the motive power—is gone.

In dramatizing the spiritual core of production, Rand challenged the ancient prejudice that material production is a mundane, mechanical, purely materialistic affair. Some of the world's major religions teach that there is a dichotomy within human nature between a higher and a lower self; and a built-in conflict between desires for materialistic, worldly goods such as wealth and physical pleasure, and aspirations for things of the spirit—knowledge, virtue, love, art, and the like. Among the Greek philosophers, Plato held to that view. And even Aristotle, who had a more worldly outlook and a more integrated, organic view of human nature, still held that man's highest and noblest activity is the exercise of reason detached from the use of it to create things in the world.

Since the Industrial Revolution and the birth of capitalism two centuries ago, the power of reason to improve human life through production has become astoundingly obvious. Yet the attitude persists even to our day. Matthew Arnold, an English writer and educator in the nineteenth century, expressed the attitude this way: "Which is more admirable, the England that produced coal and railroads, or the England that produced Shakespeare and Jonson?"

Arnold intended this as a rhetorical question: all right-thinking people would say Shakespeare and Jonson represent a more admirable achievement than the producers of coal and railroads. Rand emphatically rejects this invidious comparison as a false dichotomy. Both kinds of activity, artistic production and material producers, are forms of the human exercise of intelligence and imagination. They both take courage, integrity, and discipline. And they both add value to our world.

Now, I have been referring to material production as the creation of wealth. I want to clarify that Rand is not primarily concerned with wealth in the sense of money, cash on hand or in the bank. Rand understood her economics. Money is a measure and store of value, but the value lies in the real goods and services that have been produced. Money is also a medium of exchange, but only among those with something to trade. Money has no meaning or value if it is detached from underlying values—the real goods and services—and from the creative activities that produce them. This is what Rand means when she speaks of creating wealth, and monetary wealth that is earned through production is something to be proud of. But she is not concerned with the size of a person's bank account per se. James Taggart is a very rich man, but he acquired that money through nonproductive political manipulation—and it does him no good when his policies have destroyed the economy.

The first key to Rand's defense of capitalism, then, is that productive achievement is the essence of the human ideal, of human beings as they can be and ought to be. She is not making the economic point that capitalism excels in enabling the production of material wealth, although that is important. She is making the *ethical* point that capitalism protects and rewards those human and heroic qualities that make creation of any type possible. It protects and rewards the best within us.

THE MORALITY OF SELF-INTEREST

In the market system of capitalism, individuals pursue their self-interest. That is the basis of economic theory, but it has always posed a moral problem for defenders of capitalism because of the moral tradition of altruism.

Virtually every code of morality in history has said that helping others is a core principle of ethics, that self-sacrifice is the noblest thing a person can do, that we should all try to put service above self. If you start from that moral premise, it affects how you see the economic activities driven by self-interest: making a living, buying a house, investing in stocks, starting a company, and the like. These will seem at best amoral, but easily crossing the line into greed and avarice. Even if the overall results are beneficial, as Adam Smith showed, that fact does not change how people tend to see the individual activities. As one of Smith's predecessors, Bernard Mandeville, put it, there's a paradox in the fact that "private vice produces public benefits." So capitalism has widely been regarded as being conceived in sin. As a result, advocates of the free market tend to focus on the economic efficiency of the market and its general benefits to society.

At the same time, the critics of capitalism have always attacked it as founded on selfishness. Long before he wrote *Das Kapital*, Karl Marx was writing essays that denounced capitalism as immoral, and not just capitalists but the entire classical liberal philosophy of individual rights. For example, in "The Jewish Question," he wrote:

> None of the supposed rights of man, therefore, go beyond the egoistic man, man as he is, as a member of civil society; that is, an individual separated from the community, withdrawn into himself, wholly preoccupied with his private interest and acting in accordance with his private caprice."

Later in the nineteenth century, Beatrice Webb, a prominent member of the Fabian socialists, who pushed England to embrace the welfare state, described socialism as an attempt "to transfer the 'impulse of self-subordinating service' from God to man." It is undoubtedly this "impulse" that explains why socialism was such a popular cause. What galvanized people and made them feel socialism was an idealistic cause was not Marx's goofy economic theories. It was the idea that socialism is the *moral* ideal because it is founded on sharing, brotherhood, giving to each on the basis of need.

Today, the same altruist moral premises lie behind the frequent attacks on business and the profit motive as greedy—and behind the tendency of highly successful businesses and businessmen to feel that they must engage in philanthropy to justify the wealth they have acquired.

Rand's defense of self-interest and her criticism of the altruist morality are the most radical features of *Atlas*, illustrated in many scenes. At a crucial point in the novel, for example, Rearden is on trial for violating an arbitrary economic regulation. Instead of apologizing for his pursuit of profit or seeking mercy on the basis of philanthropy, he says: "I work for nothing but my own profit—which I make by selling a product they need to men who are willing and able to buy it. I do not produce it for their benefit at the expense of mine, and they do not buy it for my benefit at the expense of theirs; I do not sacrifice my interests to them nor do they sacrifice theirs to me; we deal as equals by mutual consent to mutual advantage—and I am proud of every penny that I have earned in this manner."

Rand held that every person is an autonomous individual, with the moral right to pursue his own happiness. She admired those who embrace the wonderful fact of their own existence and live their lives to the fullest, without guilt or apology. As she put it in the title of a later work, she believed in "the virtue of selfishness." But her conception of self-interest and egoism is radically different from the conventional picture of selfishness. It is not the kind of grasping, exploitative, attempt to satisfy urges of the moment, or seeking money, sex, and power at any cost. The villainous businessmen in *Atlas* are the ones who fit that picture. Her heroes define their self-interest by achievement, rationality, pride, and justice. In that respect, the moral philosophy of *Atlas* could just as well be described as the selfishness of virtue.

Rand took seriously the literal meaning of altruism. As she said in "Faith and Force: The Destroyers of the Modern World": "The basic principle of altruism is that man has no right to exist for his own sake, that service to others is the only justification of his existence, and that self-sacrifice is his highest moral duty, virtue, and value."[1]

---

1   As Comte put it in *A General View of Positivism*: "[The religion of Humanity] sets forth social feeling as the first principle of morality. . . . To live for others it holds to be our highest happiness. To become incorporate with humanity . . . this is what it puts before us as the constant aim of life. . . . In the positive state . . . the idea of Right will disappear. Everyone has duties, duties toward all, but Rights in

And she shows throughout the novel that sacrifice is not a moral but a highly destructive injunction. Among many other points, sacrifice as a moral imperative is the chief philosophical basis for collectivism, always invoked by the power-seekers to rationalize expropriation. And that indeed is what the strike of the producers is all about. They refuse the role of sacrificial victims. They refuse to be treated as means to the ends of others.

At the same time, the novel draws a sharp distinction between altruism and benevolence. By contrast with altruism, the spirit of benevolence leads one to help others as a choice, not a duty. It can involve giving to others in response to a temporary crisis that you can help them through, or investing in someone's potential. But it does not mean writing a blank check on one's resources to sacrifice for the endless needs of other people at large. And such benevolence does not take precedence over the virtues involved in productive achievement. It is a secondary element in morality.

There are many scenes of genuine benevolence in *Atlas*. I want to mention one in particular, because it illustrates both benevolence and altruism. Dagny is working in her private rail car on a Taggart train when she sees the conductor about to throw a bum off the train. Something about him makes Dagny think he's a good man down on his luck; she stops the conductor and ends up having a long conversation with him. Extending herself in that way is an example of Dagny's benevolent spirit. The bum tells her about a factory where he used to work, the very factory in which Dagny and Rearden had found the motor. Here's where we get to the contrast with altruism: When the founder of the company died, his three children took over and turned the place into a workers' cooperative to be run on the altruist principle "from each according to his ability, to each according to his need." The account of what happened is a brilliant analysis of what that Marxist slogan means in practice.

- ◆ In a collectivist enterprise, you cannot simply let each individual decide what his ability and needs are; that must be

the ordinary sense can be claimed by none."

decided collectively. So everyone competed to exaggerate his needs and minimize his ability.

- Decent people in such a system felt guilty about consuming too much. But those who were irresponsible, who were wasteful or profligate in spending their income and then couldn't provide for their needs, got taken care of anyway; the group provided at least the minimum.

- People were rewarded for doing a poor job, punished for doing a good one. If you did a poor job there was no penalty; you still got your needs taken care of. If you did a good job, there was no extra reward; on the contrary, you raised expectations and got more work assigned to you.

- Because of these conflicts, the system bred hatred among people, as they snooped and meddled in each other's lives to see who was slacking off work or spending money on indulgences.

- It was impossible to allocate all work and income by democratic vote. So the power to make decisions flowed into the hands of the heirs acting as economic czars over everyone's life.

- The best people left the company, refusing to work under such conditions; the quality of its product declined and customers went elsewhere.

This is what the principle of altruism comes to, finally. It is not kindness; it is not benevolence; it is not brotherly love and solidarity. The dependence of everyone on everyone else means a war of all against all, in which power rules and personal freedom, responsibility, pride, and good will are extinguished.

THE JUSTICE OF TRADE

I will turn now to the third major theme in *Atlas Shrugged*: the justice of trade.

In all of its many forms, trade is a *voluntary* interaction among people to *mutual benefit*. Both of those features are essential: Whether I am buying milk in the grocery store, hiring an employee, forming a corporation with a group of other people, buying a house, whatever, a trade is voluntary. It's something I choose to do and something that can happen only if the other party or parties also choose. And the reason we all choose it to engage in trade, of course, is that each of us expects to gain. We value what we're getting more than what we are giving in exchange, whether it's money, time, or anything else.

As a story about business, *Atlas Shrugged* highlights trade as a major type of human activity. But Rand also extends the concept beyond the realm of economic exchange, of buying and selling goods and services. Indeed, the story shows how trade in a broader sense applies to all human interactions. It applies, for example, to the exchange of ideas and information, to the marketplace of ideas, as we often say. In the realm of ideas and information, there may not be any literal transfer of possession. When I tell you something I know, I don't lose the knowledge I gave you. But it is still a voluntary interaction from which we both gain. The concept of trade even applies to personal relationships, where we give and receive emotional benefits. As Rand put the point in "The Objectivist Ethics":

> A trader is a man who earns what he gets and does not give or take the undeserved. He does not treat men as masters or slaves, but as independent equals. He deals with men by means of a free, voluntary, unforced, unco-erced exchange—an exchange which benefits both parties by their own independent judgment. . . .
>
> . . . In spiritual issues, a trader is a man who does not seek to be loved for his weaknesses or flaws, only for his virtues, and who does not grant his love to the weaknesses or the flaws of others, only to their virtues.

Rand's principle is that trade is the proper, ethical way for people to relate. "It is the principle of justice." Because it is voluntary, trade respects each individual's autonomy and freedom to act on his judgment. Forcing people to interact against their will is as hateful in the economic realm as it would be in the realm of friendship and love. The are many examples in Atlas of the government using economic coercion against the producers, regulating what they can do, depriving them of their property and of everything they had built in the expectation of being able to use it, tearing away their freedom. Rearden in particular is saddled with edicts that wreck the carefully constructed production system that had enabled him to make the best metal at the best price. These economic controls are of a piece with what totalitarian states do to artists and intellectuals by suppressing their creativity.

So the first thing that makes trade the principle of justice is that it's voluntary. The second essential feature of trade is that both parties gain. Because the benefit is mutual, individuals do not sacrifice themselves or demand sacrifices from others. Trade is just because it treats others as autonomous equals and recognizes that the values they have to offer are products of their autonomous minds. The business heroes in Atlas are fierce competitors, hard bargainers, demanding bosses. It's obvious how those attitudes reflect their pursuit of their interests. But Rand also shows how the attitudes express a deep respect for the people they are dealing with as competent to pursue their own goals and make their own decisions, without any need for pity or charity.

In speaking of equality in connection with trade, I am referring to the basic equality of people as persons, as independent, autonomous agents. I am referring to the equal dignity they deserve—or can earn —as moral beings regardless of their ability or place in life. But of course people are not equal in ability, circumstances, success, etc. And as a writer in the Romantic tradition, Rand made her heroes people of exceptional, larger-than-life talents and achievements. In this respect, there's a very important addition she makes to the principle that trade involves mutual benefit. Marx held that capitalists are exploiters because their profits are taken from revenue that would otherwise go to the workers. Many people who do not go that far are nevertheless suspicious about inequalities that occur in a free market, or feel that trade is fair only when the parties are more or less equal in bargaining position.

Rand disagrees. A key point that is explained and dramatized in *Atlas* is what she calls "the pyramid of ability." When wealth is acquired by creative achievement in a free society, those at the top of the scale in wealth provide much more value to others than they receive back; it's the people at the bottom of the scale who receive the most as return on their efforts, because their efforts are leveraged by the technology, investments, risk-taking, and management skills that went into creating the jobs they hold.

As John Galt explains:

> The man at the top of the intellectual pyr-
> amid contributes the most to all those below
> him, but gets nothing except his material pay-
> ment, receiving no intellectual bonus from
> others to add to the value of his time. The
> man at the bottom who, left to himself,
> would starve in his hopeless ineptitude, con-
> tributes nothing to those above him, but
> receives the bonus of all of their brains. Such
> is the nature of the "competition" between
> the strong and the weak of the intellect. Such
> is the pattern of "exploitation" for which you
> have damned the strong.

The antithesis of trade, and the only alternative as a way to interact with people, is *power*. Power is the effort to get something by bringing another's mind and effort under one's control, regardless of that person's choice or benefit. Power is inherently coercive, not volun-tary. It is based on the threatening the person with loss instead of offering him some gain. It is therefore a negative-sum relationship, rather than positive-sum. And where trade is a relationship between people as equals, power is a relationship of domination.

Every society has some mix of trade and power as operative principles of interaction. One of the things that makes *Atlas* a very long book is Rand's ambition to show what happens, across an entire economy—an entire society, really—as freedom to trade is replaced by the exercise of power, up to the point of collapse from a purely power-based system. The result, in my view, is a *tour de force*. It could serve as a textbook in the economics of a free market and of government intervention. Indeed, I know economists who assign the book in introductory courses for that very reason.

In the course of the narrative, we see how government actions produce unintended consequences. Price controls in one industry give rise to shortages that cascade through other industries. Regulations on who can buy Rearden Metal give rise to black markets. By the end, government has taken total control, with appointed bureaucrats making all economic decisions. With the complete abandonment of markets, we see that no rational allocation of resources is possible. In one amazing scene, Taggart freight trains are sent to Louisiana to serve some bureaucrat's pet project, so they are not available to ship a record grain harvest in Minnesota, and the wheat rots by the tracks.

Along with these economic effects, *Atlas* dramatizes the political ones. As power grows by degree, it changes its nature. It becomes increasingly arbitrary: laws are replaced by edicts, the rule of law by the whim of those in power. The pursuit of power becomes increasingly overt; the justifying fictions of serving the public interest become increasingly desperate, dishonest, and cynical. Success in business increasingly goes to political entrepreneurs—businessmen who seek wealth through political connections and manipulation—rather than real entrepreneurs who gain wealth through production. People flee from positions of responsibility in reaction to a social environment that penalizes both success and failure in unpredictable ways. To shore up its fragile, unworkable economic planning, the government becomes increasingly desperate to boost public morale by censoring critics and imposing harsh penalties for "economic crimes."

This entire story about the decline of the economy, the growth of power, and the disastrous results is a brilliant time-lapse portrayal of what happened in Soviet Russia over the course of 70 years. And many of the individual episodes read as if they were taken from yesterday's headlines. But despite the realism of her narrative, Rand's goal in *Atlas* is not primarily to make an economic or political point. Her concern is ethical: to dramatize the principle of trade as the essence of justice among people.

CONCLUSION

In telling her story about the strike of the producers and the capitalist revolution they bring about, Rand was also introducing a revolutionary moral perspective. The three core elements of that perspective, to summarize, are:

1. The glory of production, the creative nature of all productive achievement, including the creation of wealth, as opposed to the view of business as materialistic.
2. The morality of self-interest, of pursuing one's life and happiness—including the pursuit of profit, wealth, economic gain—as opposed to the morality of altruism.
3. The justice of trade as the proper relation among people, in all realms of life, as opposed to power and sacrifice.

Every social system must have some moral foundation, something to justify its political and economic prescriptions and to inspire adherents to crusade for it. In the case of socialism, the moral foundation was collectivist: the brotherhood of men, with individuals willing to sacrifice their personal interests in the service of a collective good. The moral vision of *Atlas* is the diametrical opposite in all the ways I have discussed. Rand's achievement was to present an idealistic moral case for capitalism, a case that is consistent with the actual benefits that capitalism has showered on mankind.

RAND'S PROPHETIC NOVEL

EDWARD HUDGINS

FALL 2009

S omething remarkable happened in 2009 that showed why Ayn Rand's epic novel *Atlas Shrugged* is enjoying a spike in popularity. Scores of citizens took to American streets in Tea Parties, and to town hall meetings held by elected officials, to protest the economic policies of President Obama and the Congress. It was a revolt of the producers against those who take from them by the fist of government.

Consider the signs at the demonstrations: "You cannot multiply wealth by dividing it." "Spread my work ethic, not my wealth." "Stop rewarding failure. Stop punishing success. Stop spending. Start cutting." "Don't tax what I haven't earned yet." "Cut the size of government, not our wallet." "Pro-capitalist producers, not moochers." "I'll keep my money, my freedom & my guns & you keep the 'change.'"

Many signs explicitly referenced *Atlas Shrugged*, showing that the book has helped spur this revolt.

Today, with the national debt growing to trillions of dollars and the collapse of major corporations, *Atlas Shrugged* seems prescient. In the specifics of the book we see government, controlled by alleged do-gooders, corrupt businessmen, and labor union thugs, restricting economic liberty and punishing productive individuals.

In *Atlas*, Rand depicts America's economic collapse resulting from a morality that, on its surface, sounds fine to many Americans—help others, love thy neighbor, don't be selfish. But as the story reveals, such precepts, taken seriously, have a logic all their own that drives those who accept them to destruction, taking many others with them in the process. Talk about a counter-intuitive and challenging proposition!

Accounting for *Atlas*'s popularity are scenarios strikingly similar in detail to what's happening in the world today as well as deeper insights that allow us to understand our world.

BUSINESSPEOPLE, GOOD AND BAD

The premise of *Atlas* is seen in the clear classes of heroes and villains. The world consists of producers and looters. Both classes include businesspeople, and Rand makes clear a distinction that the enemies of freedom wish to gloss over today. Some individuals grow rich by producing goods and services to satisfy the needs of willing customers and employers. This is a relationship based on *voluntary trade*. Others seek government favors, restrictions on competitors, and handouts extracted from producers. This is a relationship based upon *coercion*.

In *Atlas*, Dagny Taggart, operating vice president of Taggart Transcontinental Railroad, wants to grow rich by building new lines with cutting-edge metal tracks to meet the needs of growing enterprises. James Taggart, the company's head, wants to expropriate wealth via government mandates to restrict competitors and via moratoriums on paying back loans to the company.

Hank Rearden wants to grow rich by creating a new type of metal that is both stronger and less expensive than competing products. Steelmaker Orren Boyle wants to grow rich by having his political friends restrict the production of Rearden Metal.

In our real world today there are entrepreneurs—Bill Gates, Steve Jobs—who have created new consumer products and offered new information services that have revolutionized entertainment and communications as well as business. These are the producers, the creators of wealth.

There are also individual businessmen who try to grow rich by taking from others: Enron's Ken Lay manipulated government regulations of energy markets. American tire manufacturers and other special pleaders secure government restrictions on imports by competitors—in this case Chinese ones—so that they can charge higher prices. And let's not forget the tens of billions of taxpayer dollars handed to failed American auto companies.

BANKING ON ALTRUISM

In *Atlas*, Rand also exposes the nature of those who, rather than simply expropriating wealth, actually destroy it in the name of high moral principle. Here too the echoes with today's world are loud and clear.

For example, in the novel Eugene Lawson was president of the Community National Bank of Wisconsin. That bank collapsed because of the bad loans it made, destroying the economy of Wisconsin as well as several surrounding states. The final trigger that brought down the bank was lending to the Twentieth Century Motor Company, which Lawson knew was mismanaged and bankrupt.

In the novel Lawson explained his philosophy: "My father and grandfather built up [the bank] just to amass a fortune for themselves. I placed their fortune in the service of a higher ideal. I did not sit on piles of money and demand collateral from poor people who needed loans. The heart was my collateral."

In other words, profits are an evil end for any enterprise—or individual—to pursue; meeting the needs of others should be the goal of businesses, whether doing so brings profits or not and even if it destroys the enterprise.

Does this scenario sound familiar?

Today's banking collapses have their origin in the same morality, in most cases mandated by law as well as adopted by bankers. For example, the Community Reinvestment Act sought to force banks to make loans to the poor, even if they were poor credit risks. Indeed, CRA and Federal Reserve regulations declared that the inability to make a down payment on a house shouldn't be held against potential borrowers. Further, feds stated that government welfare received by such borrowers shouldn't count as evidence that they had little income but, rather, should be counted *as* income.

The *New York Times* reported on September 30, 1999, that "Fannie Mae, the nation's biggest underwriter of home mortgages [and a government-established enterprise], has been under increasing pressure from the Clinton Administration to expand mortgage loans among low and moderate income people." Fannie really didn't need to be pushed too hard. Many of its executives followed Lawson's morality of banking.

The *Times* article explained that Fannie had taken action "which will begin as a pilot program involving 24 banks in 15 markets—including the New York metropolitan region—[to] encourage those banks to extend home mortgages to individuals whose credit is generally not good enough to qualify for conventional loans. Fannie Mae officials say they hope to make it a nationwide program by next spring."

You know the rest of the story—bad loans in portfolios, collapsed banks, foreclosures, dried-up credit markets.

Many Americans seemed to be getting the moral lesson that Rand presents in *Atlas*. When commentator Rick Santelli did his famous February 19, 2009, rant on CNBC from the floor of the Chicago Mercantile Exchange, he asked, "How many of you people want to pay for your neighbor's mortgage that has an extra bathroom and can't pay their bills?" He called for a tea party against high taxes like the one in colonial Boston. This idea ignited the 2009 protests from coast to coast.

No doubt most Americans still have confused notions about the morality of helping the poor. But they do feel that it is unfair to penalize them, the productive people—to make them poorer—in order to help the poor. And they understand that wealth transfers from prosperous to poor in the end remove the incentive to be productive and better one's situation.

In *Atlas*, Rand depicts the human costs of such "help-the-poor" policies. In a destroyed Wisconsin town we're shown "a white-haired charwoman, moving painfully on her knees, scrubbing the steps of a house." The town's mayor explains, "They used to be solid, respectable folks. Her husband owned the dry-goods store. He worked all his life to provide for her in her old age, and he did, too, by the time he died—only the money was in the Community National Bank."

Middle-class Americans who have seen their investments disappear with the collapsing economy and fear their savings will disappear in hyperinflation brought on by massive government deficits understand that they or their children could be in the position of that charwoman as well. No wonder *Atlas Shrugged* hits home!

THE "ARISTOCRACY OF PULL"

In *Atlas* Rand does a masterful job of showing the process by which raw political power—the aristocracy of pull—replaces individual productive activities and free exchange as the means for determining who gets what. Dire consequences follow.

The government agents take up residence in corporate offices to make sure that businesses are following political dictates. The loathsome Cuffy Meigs is the pol who pulls the strings at Taggart Transcontinental to get favors for his friends. Rand no doubt was thinking of the political model of the Soviet Union from which she fled, where Communist Party officials were assigned to every enterprise—owned by the government anyway—to make certain that managers strictly followed party dictates.

The Obama administration has taken up this model in practice. It has insisted on assigning its own political friends to the boards of the auto companies—e.g. General Motors—and banks that it has bailed out or taken over.

In *Atlas* an unelected and unaccountable bureaucrat, former lobbyist Wesley Mouch (aided by bank destroyer Lawson in a new, political job) essentially is made economic dictator as head of the Bureau of Economic Planning and National Resources.

Under Obama we have by one count 32 "czars" who are not elected and who, for the most part, are not approved by Congress. Many have wide, extra-constitutional powers. Among them there are an Auto Recovery Czar, Car Czar, California Water Czar, Climate Czar, Economic Czar, Energy and Environment Czar, Green Jobs Czar, Health Czar, Information Czar, Pay Czar, Regulatory Czar, Troubled Assets Relief Program Czar, and Technology Czar. Obama certainly has a preference for the worst from Russia!

RANDIAN VILLAIN

The behavior of one current congressional creature is like a composite of Randian political villains. Rep. Barney Frank (D-MA) was one of the principals facilitating Fannie's "help-the-poor" policies and protecting it from other policy-makers who feared it would collapse under its bad loans and require huge taxpayer bailouts. Frank's lover for many years was Fannie executive Herb Moses—can you say conflict of interest? In June 2009, only months before the banks crashed, Frank was pressuring Fannie to liberalize lending for the purchase of condominiums.

When Fannie and many other banks holding bad loans that it facilitated collapsed, Frank spewed out the moral indignation of a bully. He hauled bank executives—though not his friends—before congressional committees where he denounced them for their greed and threatened them with punitive government action. He also demanded government control of corporate salaries.

The sleazy, hypocritical politicians found in the pages of *Atlas* are seen in all their moral ugliness in the halls of Congress today. No wonder *Atlas* is so popular again.

FROM STARNESVILLE TO DETROIT

Businesses fail during any economic downturn. But *Atlas Shrugged* depicts a kind of economic carnage that, until today, was hardly imaginable by most Americans.

Rand describes Starnesville, the home of the Twentieth Century Motor Company, formerly one of the country's biggest and best enterprises. The company was destroyed by its founder's heirs, who ran the business on the socialist principle, "From each according to his ability, to each according to his need."

Here's one of the descriptions of the once motor Mecca:

"A few houses still stood within the skeleton of what had once been an industrial town. Everything that could move, had moved away; but some human beings had remained. The empty structures were vertical rubble; they had been eaten, not by time but by men; boards torn out at random, missing patches of roofs, holes left in gutted cellars."

Many American cities today have declined past the point of simply being dangerous, rundown, but populated ghettoes. They've become depopulated. Take the train from Baltimore heading north and you'll look back on abandoned blocks of boarded up houses. Drive through parts of St. Louis and you'll encounter urban deserts.

With the collapse of General Motors and Chrysler, the fate of Detroit is like something out of *Atlas Shrugged*. That city has become so de-industrialized that the Sustainable Development Assessment Team, headed by Alan Mallach, suggests huge swaths of abandoned areas simply be bulldozed. The *Detroit Free Press* reports that "in a new vision of Detroit's future, a team of visiting urban planners suggests the city might one day resemble the English countryside, with distinct urban villages surrounded by farms, fields, and meadows."

A once-great industrial city will sink back into the earth, covered by a landscape of little farms and grazing animals. It's Rome after its fall, with the Forum covered by weeds and mud and the remains of basilicas serving as cow barns.

PRODUCTIVE PEOPLE SHRUG

The title of Rand's great opus is a prediction about what will happen if governments continue with policies that penalize the productive and a warning about what would happen if all productive individuals who are damned for being productive cease to "inflict" their competence on an ungrateful world. We've seen the predictions come true.

In past decades businesses have moved from states with high taxes and heavy-handed government regulations to those that place less of a burden on the productive, for example, from California to Nevada and Arizona. More businesses likely will shut their doors entirely or relocate overseas if Obama's punitive environmental regulations threaten to drain their capital and revenues.

In recent years medical doctors have grown sick of having their wealth drained away in nuisance lawsuits by predatory lawyers—big-time donors to the Democratic Party—facilitated by government. Many have periodically gone on strike for tort reform. Many specialists at the peak of their talents have retired early out of frustration with government restrictions and paperwork. And in a September 2009 *Investor's Business Daily*/TIPP survey, four out of nine doctors said they "would consider leaving their practice or taking an early retirement" if Congress passed Obamacare.

We see even more obvious indications today that productive people are voting with their feet. A May 27, 2009, story in the *Washington Examiner* reported that the number of high-income taxpayers in the high-tax state of Maryland had dropped by one-third over the prior year.

The U.S. government has brought bogus criminal charges against Swiss interests in the United States in order to pressure the Swiss to turn over information about so-called "tax evaders." And so many productive individuals are fleeing their own countries to escape confiscatory government policies that the Obama administration and major Western European governments are targeting "tax havens" in Switzerland.

It's like something out of *Atlas Shrugged*.

ABSOLUTELY UNREAL

Atlas has a currency that goes beyond its parallels with American politics today. Rand shines a light on a more fundamental cause of the country's problems that is so obvious and ever-present that, remarkably, most people until now have ignored it even as it was killing them.

We all understand that politicians spin the facts to suit their agendas. That's been going on since the ancient Greeks both created and abused the art of rhetoric. But we assume that despite the "show," politicians can actually distinguish, in their own minds, facts from fairy tales.

In *Atlas*, Rand's villains at first sound like typical politicians, but soon it becomes clear that they believe their own lies. At a certain level they know that they are *lying to themselves*, that they are ignoring objective reality. They know this because it is an effort to evade facts. They have to work at it. Ultimately they want to believe that if they close their minds and blank out uncomfortable facts, the world will simply change to meet their whims.

In one scene government dictators explain to steel magnate Hank Rearden how they intend to save his industry as a whole—read his incompetent competitor—through a Steel Unification Plan. All income from steel producers will be placed into a common pool and distributed to manufacturers based on how many furnaces each company owns. Follow the math here for a moment as an incredulous Rearden explains their own plan to them:

"Orren Boyle's Associated Steel owns 60 open-hearth furnaces, one-third of them standing idle and the rest producing an average of 300 tons of steel per furnace per day. I own 20 open-hearth furnaces, working at capacity, producing 750 tons of Rearden Metal per furnace per day. So we own 80 'pooled' furnaces with a 'pooled' output of 27,000 tons, which makes an average of 337.5 tons per furnace. Each day of the year, I producing 15,000 tons, will be paid for 6,750 tons.

Boyle, producing 12,000 tons, will be paid for 20,250 tons. . . . Now how long do you expect me to last under your plan?"

Rearden can't believe that these bureaucrats *actually* believe such nonsense. And their only answers are: "In time of national peril, it's your duty to serve" and, "You have to make certain sacrifices to the public welfare" and, "You'll manage."

THINK THIS IS FICTION?

Many Americans were incredulous when President Obama's 2009 spending was projected to run a deficit of $1.8 trillion, with projected deficits over the next decade reaching over $9 trillion. The administration, in Orwellian language, called much of this spending "investments." Where on earth was the money going to come from?

On top of this, Obama pushed universal, government-guaranteed health care as a means to *reduce* government spending. He proposed to heap new goodies on millions of recipients as a means to lower costs and promised not to reduce any services to the elderly under Medicare. The Congressional Budget Office said such a proposal would add another $1 trillion in new government spending.

Obama claimed he'd be able to pay for a substantial part of the new spending by squeezing the waste and fraud out of Medicare. One might ask how he thinks a government that allows such a huge amount of waste in one major program will be able to run a new program any better. In any case the only way to reduce Medicare costs by such a huge amount would be to cut services.

Some of Obama's minions suggest that new taxes on the "rich" or on pharmaceutical companies could cover a sizable chunk of this spending. But even a 100 percent tax rate on the top five percent of taxpayers would bring in only a fraction of what would be needed to meet Obama's spending plans.

More and more Americans are asking, "Can these guys really believe their own b.s.? Surely they wouldn't be so grossly, almost criminally irresponsible as to destroy the American economy and current healthcare system with such a plan?" The answer, of course, is "Yes they can."

AN EYE-OPENER

Atlas offers us a way to understand the level of self-delusion we see in the world today. Rand understood that the root of all evil is first and foremost the refusal to think, the refusal to focus one's mind, the evasion of reality. It might start with individuals deceiving others but, ultimately, it ends in individuals deceiving themselves. It might start in small matters but such a practice in the end can lead to destruction on a national level.

Americans who turned to *Atlas* because of its parallels to America's politics and economics will discover this deepest of moral insights, which offers a guide for creating the personal morality that is a prerequisite for the culture necessary to support political and economic freedom.

A morality of rational self-interest must start with the "rational" part. Most Americans do have a strong streak of self-interest, of concern for themselves, their own careers, well-being, friends, and loved ones. Most have a morality of "help one's self" and "earn one's way." Most have a common-sense approach to understanding the world. They have their eyes open.

Atlas Shrugged is a novel that offers an integrated philosophy that builds on the best in the American culture. It gives Americans a light for seeing clearly that fine-sounding platitudes about helping one's neighbor can lead to dire consequences—and destroy one's poor neighbor in the process.

The popularity of *Atlas* today offers an opportunity for Americans not only to reverse the slide toward tyranny, but to build an even stronger polity of freedom and culture of productive achievement.

Atlas Libertas *and its creator*

ATLAS LIBERTAS

A*tlas Libertas*, shown opposite and on the front cover, is a high-relief sculpture on the main façade of the business school at the Universidad Francisco Marroquín in Guatemala City. It was unveiled in October 2007, on the fiftieth anniversary of *Atlas Shrugged*. On the dedication plaque is a passage from Galt's speech.

"In my recreation of Atlas," says the sculptor, Walter Peter Brenner, as quoted on the university website, "it is not the mythological figure I represent, but a metaphorical one in the form of a human being, the individual mover of human development . . . a capable, strong, just, ambitious, and intelligent human who requires individual freedom in order to reach his highest potential. It is, thus, Rand's heroic vision of man that I want to express: a person who through his essential virtues remains true to his highest values, struggling to achieve his goals without violating the individual rights of his fellow man."

RESOURCES

FURTHER READINGS BY AYN RAND

THE FOUNTAINHEAD. Through the careers of two architects, one who devotes himself to his vision of architecture and one who quickly rises to fame and wealth, Rand's penultimate novel explores what it means—and what it doesn't mean—to live for yourself.

WE THE LIVING. This novel—the closest thing Rand said she'd ever write to an autobiography—tells the story of an ambitious young woman trapped in Soviet Russia.

THE VIRTUE OF SELFISHNESS. In this collection of essays, Rand lays out the foundations of her ethics—beginning with the question, "*Why* does man need a code of values?"—and her politics.

CAPITALISM: THE UNKNOWN IDEAL. In these essays, Rand and others expound on individual rights and answer attacks on freedom.

PHILOSOPHY: WHO NEEDS IT. Key essays in this volume include a case for studying philosophy and a debunking of the idea of duty.

THE ROMANTIC MANIFESTO. The philosopher-novelist gives her philosophy of art in this collection of essays.

VIDEO RESOURCES FROM THE ATLAS SOCIETY

ATLAS UNIVERSITY SCENE COMMENTARIES. In these videos, David Kelley draws out the philosophical meanings of specific scenes from the *Atlas Shrugged* movies. http://www.atlassociety.org/atlas-shrugged-course

OBJECTIVISM: A RATIONAL PHILOSOPHY FOR THE HERO IN YOUR SOUL. In this video series, based on a one-day course prepared for the Atlas Summit, Alexander R. Cohen gives a systematic overview of the Objectivist philosophy. http://www.atlassociety.org/orphys

ATLAS UNIVERSITY COURSE ON REASON. Objectivism is a philosophy based on reason, but what is reason? David Kelley and William R Thomas discuss the choice to think, the nature of concepts, and other related issues. http://www.atlassociety.org/atlas-university-reason

ATLAS SUMMIT VIDEOS. At our annual gathering, a diverse range of speakers extend and apply the Objectivist philosophy in areas such as politics, work, family life, psychology, and art. Then we publish most of the lectures as videos. http://www.atlassociety.org/as/

FURTHER READING FROM THE ATLAS SOCIETY

WHAT IS OBJECTIVISM? This set of online articles by William R Thomas is a short, clear overview of Rand's key ideas. It covers topics from the nature of philosophy and why one needs it to the nature of art. http://www.atlassociety.org/what_is_objectivism

MYTHS ABOUT AYN RAND. In this short book, David Kelley and William R Thomas explain what's wrong with some popular misconceptions of Ayn Rand's views.

The Atlas Society offers many additional articles and videos about *Atlas Shrugged* on its website, as well as original research in Objectivism; commentary applying Objectivism to current issues in politics, culture, and law; and applications of the philosophy to work and personal life. http://www.atlassociety.org.

AUTHORS

ROBERT BIDINOTTO is author of the bestselling fiction thrillers *Hunter* and *Bad Deeds*. He first became acquainted with Ayn Rand's works in 1967, as a college freshman. His subsequent career as an award-winning journalist, editor, and novelist has been heavily influenced by Rand's philosophy and literature. Besides novels, Bidinotto also authored two nonfiction books about the criminal justice system. His wide-ranging articles, essays, and reviews have appeared in numerous publications, including *Reader's Digest*, *The Boston Herald*, and *The American Spectator*. One of his investigative articles for *Reader's Digest* was a National Magazine Award finalist and is widely credited as having influenced the outcome of the 1988 presidential election. As editor of *The New Individualist*, former magazine of The Atlas Society, Bidinotto received the Folio Gold "Eddie" Award, the magazine industry's highest honor. He lives with his wife on Maryland's Chesapeake Bay, where he writes fiction full-time. He can be contacted through his website: http://www.bidinotto.com.

JOAN CARTER is co-founder of UM Holdings Ltd. During the 40 years since she and John Aglialoro founded the company, UM has been involved in a wide variety of business ventures. It currently owns Cybex International, a manufacturer of commercial fitness equipment, and

EHE International, a provider of physical examinations to corporate employees. She is a graduate of the College of Wooster, a former chairman of the board of the Philadelphia Federal Reserve, a member of the board of Penn Mutual Life Insurance Company, and a director of FreedomWorks, a grassroots organization promoting free markets and individual liberty. As the wife of producer John Aglialoro, Carter has been involved in the *Atlas Shrugged* movie trilogy since its inception and is associate producer for *Part III*.

ALEXANDER R. COHEN, associate scholar at The Atlas Society, edited the bestselling *Myths about Ayn Rand* and blogs for the Business Rights Center. He has lectured on a variety of topics in Objectivist ethics and politics. He has degrees in philosophy, law, and journalism.

EDWARD HUDGINS is director of advocacy and a senior scholar at The Atlas Society, where he has also served as executive director. He's worked as director of regulatory studies for the Cato Institute and editor of *Regulation* magazine. He was a senior economist for the Joint Economic Committee of Congress and was both deputy director for economic policy studies and director of the Center for International Economic Growth at the Heritage Foundation. His commentaries have appeared in major national publications, and he's appeared on major TV and radio news shows. His most recent book is *The Republican Party's Civil War: Will Freedom Win?* Hudgins has a doctorate in political philosophy.

DAVID KELLEY, founder and chief intellectual officer of The Atlas Society, earned his Ph.D. in philosophy from Princeton University in 1975 and later taught cognitive science and philosophy at Vassar College and Brandeis University. His articles on social issues and public policy have appeared in *Harpers*, *Reason*, *Harvard Business Review*, the *Freeman*, and elsewhere. His books include *Unrugged Individualism: The Selfish Basis of Benevolence*; *The Contested Legacy of Ayn Rand: Truth and Toleration in Objectivism*; *The Evidence of the Senses*; and *The Art of Reasoning*, one of the most widely used logic textbooks in the country.

Made in the USA
Columbia, SC
06 February 2018